IM PRESS

Евсей Цейтлин

ПЕРЕЧИТЫВАЯ МОЛЧАНИЕ

Из дневников этих лет

Yevsey Tseytlin

REREADING SILENCE

From the Diaries of Those Years

Translated by Venya Gushchin

Boston • 2025 • Chicago

Yevsey Tseytlin   Rereading Silence
From the Diaries of Those Years

Translated by Venya Gushchin

Second edition, corrected and updated

ISBN 978-1950319978
Library of Congress Control Number: 2023932963

Published by M·Graphics | Boston, MA
   ☐ www.mgraphics-books.com
   ✉ mgraphics.books@gmail.com

In cooperation with Bagriy & Company | Chicago, IL
   ☐ www.bagriycompany.com
   ✉ printbookru@gmail.com

Book Design by Yuliya Timoshenko © 2025
Cover Design by Larisa Studinskaya © 2023

Cover design based on Fayum mummy portrait
Public Domain, *Wikimedia.org*

Yevsey Tseytlin's photography by Rimantas Dichavicius

Printed in the United States of America

Table of Contents

Not Remembering it All

From the Cycle "The Experience of Parting"

The Calm Fortitude of His Prose

Any one of Yevsey Tseytlin's books is taken in as an entire universe—a universe of intertwining fates, emotions, thoughts, and dreams. These books are to be read slowly because a cursory glance is impossible. Every episode, every memory, and every face forcefully bring the reader back to the words on the page, to make sense of them and their inner gaze. That's why the characters of this prose are so memorable, so numerous that they could comprise a city. There's not a single passing thought, not a single banal observation, not a single divergent fate.

Troubling and quarrelsome, wise and profound, lucky and unlucky—the characters in these books remind the reader of old photographs. The subjects would prepare, sitting for a long time, tense and immobile, all so that the picture would come out well, so that their faces would be preserved forever: for their grandkids, their great-grandkids. That's why it feels like they're looking out at us, observing us and our contemporary world with that typical exacting expression you see in photographs of the past. In this ability lies the author's extraordinary powers of rapt attention; his ability to look into the depths of life; his skill at noticing and fishing out the painful and piercing essence of history, individual scenes and situations, and fates. That essence is precious, grabbing us living today, however overwhelmed and bustling we may be. Grabbing us and never letting go.

But the most important part of these essays and miniatures is tone. In any book the most important thing is tone. In Yevsey Tseyltin's prose, the tone is of calm fortitude.

Dina Rubina

The Lonely Ones
Among Pedestrians

They had a particular look in their eyes. It seemed to me they even had a particular smell. And for sure, a particular gait.

Theirs was the gait of lonely people.

They instantly caught my attention—many years ago, when I had just begun to write down the life stories of Soviet Jews.

Sometimes it was only a light splash of words and gestures— uneven confessions coming out like hurried breath in the lines at the American and Dutch consulates (the latter had long represented the Jewish state in Moscow)—then at the Israeli consulate.

Overcoming their fear, they would come for visits and visas. After a while I would recognize them, made friends with some.

But many got lost, disappeared somewhere. Only their faces and voices still reside in my notepad.

Without a Language

A motionless, almost frozen face. There is an obvious contrast with the anguished, halting words I hear.

"You'll never guess why I hate the "Pamyat" society[1] ..." She pauses, but I don't really feel like guessing. Regardless, I would never be able to come to the same conclusion as her: "I can't stand the fact that I'm obligated to use the same language as them!"

She catches the look of surprise on my face: "I don't mean that in any figurative sense: no, literally—I converse, think, read, dream only in Russian."

She is hysterical, mostly just listening to herself talk. However, though she is wrong, she unwittingly approaches the truth.

"They... they despise me. They despise my very being. And I have no choice but to use the same language as them. They say that Jews are getting the Russian people hooked on alcohol—that they've already destroyed village life, ruined culture. Is this demagoguery? But here's their best argument: I answer them using their own language. What do I have that's my own, that's really Jewish? I'm completely barren, just a rootless tumbleweed..."

I remain silent, scared to agree with her, to pour salt in the wound. Yet I know that almost everything that's been said here is true... Of course, in her head there's a mix of the books that she's read: Remarque, Hemmingway, Kafka, Bulgakov... At different times these authors were fashionable, each one briefly held her interest. But really, Yesenin is one she truly loves: she feels the anguish of the soul that hides behind his poor rhymes, similes like "my head flaps its ears, like a bird flaps its wings." It would seem that she feels a closeness to his reckless sincerity, his ebb-less flow of confessions.

At the post office on Bolshaya Ordynka street someone asks me:

"Do you have a pen on you?"

Then, recognizing me as one of "her own," she adds:

"I need to write down my information to get an invitation from Israel. You came here for the same thing, right?"

No further explanation needed. We simply walk over to the Israeli consulate, and she drops her envelope in the mailbox. Then we stand among those waiting outside, listening to their conversations looping like a broken record. We walk back to the metro, inhaling the rare scents of spring.

"Everyone goes to Israel for their children, but I haven't got any... never going to have any..."

Only a few short, sudden, seemingly random phrases. But I can already picture her woeful, crumpled-up life that appears to have already flown by.

She is forty-nine, but looks younger: this happens at times to women that have given up on themselves. Her thick red hair is contained by a black band. She doesn't seem to be at all embarrassed that there's an oil stain on her dark blue coat, that her grey shoes are scratched on the sides.

She teaches at the technical institute. The last few years, noticing her own lack of restraint, she still manages to learn to be measured at work: to be quiet, to appear productive and together. But this skill, hard to acquire in the first place, melted away in February like she had never learned it at all. Yes, in February of 1990, when the agonizing fear of pogroms was felt in Moscow and other major cities.

Those days when her thoughts were consumed by one thing only, she spent half a class talking about anti-semitism. The students watched her in shock. And, of course, one of them informed the principal. He called her into his office and spoke, cringing and squeezing out his words, though not, as she expected, about her being fired—he asked her to not "get off topic in class" again.

We say goodbye at the metro and exchange phone numbers for some reason. It's obvious that we will never call each other. And now she vanishes into the flow of legs and elbows, into the smell of sweat and grocery bags, into the din of that speech she now despises and, later in life, will have a hard time learning not to miss.

Jewish Luck

A wet day in March, gloomy since the morning. The same humming crowd as yesterday. spitting out the same words like sunflower seed shells: luggage... tickets... pogrom...

Now a new little word falls from the heavens: lucky.

Am I hallucinating? But the next day and the day after I hear the same words of envy: Jews have it good now!

Sometimes they communicate this only in their intonation, in their gaze: Russians, Ukrainians, Georgians—all of them carried over here by their dreams of leaving.

Ah, what an old, cliched joke! "A Jewess for a wife isn't a luxury, she's a way out." I'm sure you've heard. People will pay big money for a fake marriage.

Of course, I still shudder whenever I hear: "We're the lucky ones..."

That little word melts in the mouth of a young Jewish man from Baku like a piece of Turkish delight. Smiling, clearly enjoying the attention of the passersby asking him to give details of the recent pogrom in Baku[2].

"We're the lucky ones... They gave Armenians a year to get out of the city, Jews got three. And the Russians? Five years..."

I don't know if that's true. Probably just rumors. But I wasn't thinking about the factual accuracy of his claims, but about the humiliating joy that radiated from him. This joy has ancient roots: knowing that he is on the second-to-lowest rung of the food chain raises a Jew's spirits—at least he's not at the bottom.

That Same Day—Another Meeting

Another pair from Baku. Also young, newlyweds.

A mysterious union from time immemorial: an Armenian and a Jew. It's as if they got married without any fear of multiplying the eternal sorrows of their respective peoples.

During the pogrom they hid with an Azerbaijani family for a week, but that's too common a story among refugees to tell it now in great detail: the trembling at the sound of each ring of the doorbell; the stuffy air of the pantry where they hid, lost in guessing what's happening outside; finally, plane tickets ("we paid six times their price!"); now staying in Moscow with distant relatives...

"What would happen if you got caught?" someone asks.

The husband shrugs—he doesn't want to pile the weight of his words onto anyone.

The wife responds:

"The very least—they'd cut our ears off... we had nightmares about that, night after night."

She looks to the side, the others in line keep staring at her. She's frail, like a miniature portrait. Despite her living situation being in flux, her hair is very neatly coiffed. She looks very elegant in her fuzzy black pants, white leather boots, and white nylon coat. All of this is for her husband's sake, of course. She doesn't know that she looks like her sisters out of the Bible—young naïve girls that grow into wise old women. But I can tell that she's aware that her happy eyes are out of place here in this crowd. That's why she always lowers her gaze, trying to hide all the things that are obvious to anyone paying attention: her tenderness, her determination to outsmart fate, her calm acceptance of the bitter road ahead, the road that awaits us all.

1991, the line outside the American embassy

One Small Detail

How do I quickly paint her portrait? Stout; perhaps, grand, majestic, I would say. She clearly figured out her answers to all of life's questions a long time ago.

That's exactly what old Jewish women are often like.

Now she's insistently telling someone with a dull and curious bitterness in her voice:

"...No, you have no idea what assholes those Israelis are! You can't even imagine it... They've raised a generation that has no hope of building any sort of future... You'll see, you'll believe me, I only need one small detail to see the whole."

So, what is this "one small detail"?

It turns out, the detail was a performance of an Israeli amateur theater group that recently took place in Vilnius. More precisely, it was the sight of two young actors kissing, a boy and girl (in the intermission they were kissing "in front of everyone" — sitting on a bench right outside of the theater).

After talking to the old woman, I completely understand her annoyance.

Of course, she's annoyed at herself. Or at the absurdity of life? It's been three days since she's put in her application at the visa office, together with her son's family.

1990, Vilnius

The One Who Stays

Not many of them will stay. More accurately: it's their fear that will stay. Once fear has set up residence in your soul, it's hard to defeat it.

Moses commanded the Jews living in Egypt to leave their homes immediately and set off. Out of slavery. To the Promised Land.

Why the hurry? Not because Moses was scared of the pharaoh pursuing them. He was well aware of the real danger: if he delayed their journey even a bit, the Jews themselves would have grown hesitant.

...Only twenty percent of our ancestors followed Moses out of Egypt. The majority stayed.

Snow on Saturday

Today it is deserted here: it's Saturday. Today Jews are supposed to be thinking about eternity, dismissing all the paltry bustle of everyday life. Snow falls quietly on the sidewalk. The pedestrians are few, so the snow doesn't turn into a squelching mush like it does during the week. It's warm. And the police officer at the consulate doesn't hide in his booth. Pacing around the metal detector, he's sunk into his own thoughts.

Now and then people still walk up to the entrance. They read the announcements posted on the concrete wall, which are strange because they are so ordinary: phone numbers and addresses of moving companies, the guidelines for reserving tickets, ads for available apartments. The people who come up write down the relevant information and then go their separate ways.

At midday an old Jewish man stops by for a while. He's taken the morning train from a Moscow suburb. He was told that the consulate is open every day, and, like almost everyone in Russia, he had forgotten Jewish law and had come on the Sabbath. He can't bring himself to approach the police officer, the only one there. Finally, he asks:

"Excuse me, are any of the diplomats from Israel here today?"

"It's their day off... on Saturday they're not supposed to work..." the officer says knowledgeably.

"Yes, yes," the old man hops from one foot to the other. And again, unexpectedly overcomes his shyness:

"I was told that I could give my information for an invite for permanent residence..."

"You can," the office confirms, "If you want, give me your documents and put the envelope into a special box."

The old man remains silent: how can he trust a goy, and a police officer at that? He's clearly been placed here to collect information for the state; but what choice does the old man have? Come here again? He gazes at the police officer with a questioning look in his eyes. The officer is in his early twenties. His eyes are bright, his cheeks big and child-like.

I'm standing with my back to them, looking at the bulletin board. Neither one pays any attention to me. And now the old man leaps towards me—joyfully. He immediately pegged me as Jewish based on my appearance. And the envelope that he had prepared is shaking in his hand:

"Could you take a look, please... is everything in order?"

He covers part of the page with his palm, protecting it from the snow and from the officer's eyes. I first take notice of his birthyear: 1910. I also see that there's only one surname listed. That means he's going alone. But the old man's thoughts are elsewhere. He asks the officer about the procedures around getting documents in order, about sending over luggage. The officer turns out to be very much on top of everything (during his shifts, his mind has recorded all the repetitive conversations of the consulate visitors). And for some reason this doesn't surprise the old man.

We stand, slowly enveloped by snowflakes. Then the old man starts looking for something in the windows of the empty stores. Slowly, carefully, without any extraneous movements, he glides on the snow in his antediluvian boots. I remember about thirty years we used to call those kinds of boots "farewell, youth."

1989

Their Truth

I was always fascinated by anti-Semites — their fates, their hatred that steadily grows stronger over the years, their burning "truth," wherein logical connections are peculiarly tangled up.

In the Baltic city of Kaliningrad, on the Leningrad Prospect, an old woman walks towards me, carrying heavy bags. She wears a beret on her head and a long, woven scarf droops behind and in front of her old coat. (These are the typical, naïve attempts of the intelligentsia to hide how poor they are).

I notice from afar how mercilessly the November wind whips at her slight frame.

Meeting my gaze, she walks over to me. She stops, lowers her bags, and proclaims, clearly enunciating every word:

"...And it's all the Jews' fault!"

And, having uttered this "sacred truth," the woman slowly continues on her way.

1989, November

Phrases

Those who come *from over there* all tell the same story: no one could believe their eyes upon discovering on arrival that everyone around them was Jewish. And I can confirm: this feeling is incomparable. Trust me, you start breathing differently! Literally, breathing there is easier. After all, we're all compressed, bound up back here...

Whom do these words belong to? Doesn't matter! Every time someone will let them slip out while waiting in line. Someone who is going to Israel for the second or third time. A lady from Minsk, a hair dresser from Voronezh, a retiree from Bălți...

Sometimes, however, you hear something different. Either with a giggle or completely seriously:

"...Israel is great, but so many Jews!"

These phrases can essentially be voiced by one and the same person. Of course, at different times and with different intonations.

You might try asking: why? Most likely, the one voicing it can't really explain. And I myself won't try to explain it right now: it would take too long. But if you think about it, you'll come to understand it yourself—what two thousand years of diaspora have done to us.

1992, January

A Map

A chance encounter, as always. I meet him in an apartment in Moscow, where he arrives straight from the train station. He is from Saratov. Our mutual friends had brought over a letter from his Israeli relatives. And in the envelope—easy enough to guess—is an invitation for "permanent residence."

I can picture him even now. He's lounging on a rocking chair: after a careless movement his dusty, thick-soled low shoes jump up sharply. His pants are wrinkled, and he wears brown synthetic socks. He is very cautious and shy and as a result rarely appears at ease. Even the question "do you want some coffee?" leaves him baffled.

He knows that it's just a polite gesture (his hosts are rushing off somewhere), but he can't refuse — so he drinks two cups, devouring an entire plate of sandwiches ("Sorry, I'll just take one more." "Well, of course, of course").

He doesn't say anything else. Words cake him in a thick layer, as if they're covering up something important. However, he has nothing to hide, which becomes apparent after a few minutes. Of course, he has no idea why he had decided to leave: "This is beyond logic." Finally, at the age of forty-two, he defended his dissertation, got the position of senior research fellow at the institute, and decided to build a dacha. "Anti-Semitism is real, of course, but no one's really harmed me..."

All of this is typical, so I've stopped listening to him (I haven't learned anything about his parents whom he still lives with).

I'm listening to the Okudzhava songs come in from the room next door — the kid's room — and keep looking at B.

He could be considered cute, but his thick red beard doesn't suit him at all — it really clashes with the anxious look in his eyes. Typically, a beard gives a face a sense of closure, of completeness — he, on the hand, is absent-mindedness embodied. Maybe that's why never leaves, overstays his welcome, seems to require some sort of hint to leave...

When I see him again — again completely accidentally — it's on the Bolshaya Ordynka, and B seems to be even more wrinkled than before. He's living in a hostel (a room with four beds), clearly hasn't showered in days: through his coat, I can see a clean shirt he has gotten out of his Saratov suitcase, but his hair is glossy, and dandruff lines his collar.

At the consulate he walks from group to group impatiently. In his eyes I can see the same expectation: someone — but who? — has to answer all his doubts.

He's happy to see me (an old friend!) and quickly invites me to grab a bite at a basement café. We walk there for a while: like every person from the provinces, B knows that there are only a few fairly priced buffet-style restaurants in Moscow. At the café he hoists two portions of sausage, a plate of dinner rolls, two cups of weak coffee with condensed milk onto his tray. And he just keeps on talking like he doesn't want to listen to his inner voice—or perhaps he's trying to block this quiet voice out.

Afterwards we sit on a bench. He lights a cigarette and produces a map of Israel, bought from a scalper, out of his bag. Lips moving like a kid sounding words out, he reads the ancient names printed atop the landscape out loud. I think to myself: millions of people have pronounced these combinations of phonemes with trepidation for thousands of years. And these phonemes are completely unreal to him.

Finally, he falls silent and looks past me, off to the side.

1990

A Talent
for Disappearing

"Survival is essential. And in order to survive, you have to re-main unnoticed. This is the lesson that the one who is beaten often is forced to learn... Jews have to wear a mask, to absorb the local language, to become actors in order to look like everyone around them."

* * *

"Life in the diaspora is like the lot of the pretender: it often leads you to become one with your mask, forgetting what your own face looks like."

Rabbi Adin Steinsaltz[3]

An Old Question

A completely, definitively summer evening covers over the bustle of the day. But then a four-year-old boy will come fly-ing into the room from the street. It will be imperative for him to know the truth—immediately:

"Mama, are we really Jewish?"

"Yes," she will manage to respond.

She will want to follow up with something more dignified: Jews are a people like any other, all peoples are equal... But first she will pat her son on the hand and press him close to her! The boy, however, will sharply pull himself away from her and cast aside not only his mother's hand, but all the words she does not say. A child's intuition is more accurate than any words. He intuits the most important part of this question perfectly. He has come to feel this most important part by listening to the tone of the jokes and isolated comments told around the neighborhood even though he hadn't understood their meaning. But he is sure that he gets it. And he's afraid, though he's not yet sure what of.

Still the son will look into her eyes with hope:

"Mama, is there really nothing we can do about it? Nothing we can do to fix it?"

She will tell me about this conversation fifteen years later, a few months ago. And now I constantly think back to it: what conclusions did he come to, when he realized that there was nothing that could be done "to fix it"?

The conclusions have been the same since time immemorial.

As a young boy he would amaze everyone with his generosity: he was still in kindergarten when he started giving away everything, whether it was appropriate as a gift or not. And this was not merely a matter of his compassionate heart: he wanted to turn every passerby into a friend, no matter the cost. And he manages to do so—he manages to guess other people's weaknesses, easily come into other people's lives. Two years ago, he started university as a physics major and is already giving serious talks as part of the student science society.

Does he articulate a clear vision for himself? I don't know. But I can tell what it might be: a myriad of friends, an academic career, as well as karate (he's been doing it since eighth grade)—all of which will help him become at least "not worse than others."

I've met him at a café twice, hanging out with a group of his peers. I observed him briefly, only from afar—so that he wouldn't notice me and get uncomfortable. He was very elegant in the typical uniform of youth fashion in those days—a black t-shirt and dickies. He was handsome—the kind of handsomeness that annoys some and attracts others: matte-like skin; bright blue-gray eyes; dark wavy hair. He was always at ease, always had a joke ready, albeit a crass one at times.

"Isn't it strange?" I asked myself. I had grown used to seeing him completely focused on numerous affairs, both his own and others', carefully scratching out in his notepad the execution of a daily plan. Of course, he always draws up these plans himself. He had long stopped asking his parents for advice despite, I am sure, loving them tenderly, if a bit condescendingly, as if he possessed some knowledge they had no access to. That's why he sometimes looks older than his age — as if weighed down by the seriousness and finality of the future.

I remember when the phone would ring, he'd be the first to snatch up the receiver and transform — like a sharp winter gust of Siberian wind had torn into the two-bedroom apartment with low ceilings. "So, well, what's the situation?" he'd say energetically. These words — a conventional signal to himself — a signal that was meant to elicit a conventional reflex.

He'd turn to face the wall and — I could tell by his voice — become a happy-go-lucky, free young man again.

...He is still quite varied, not yet fully formed as a person.

When he opens the door for me, I look into his eyes — and there I see the inextinguishable melancholy, a typically Jewish readiness to understand everyone, to make everyone get along, to find one's own truth in everything.

I shake his hand and think: what will he tell his son in response to that same old question?

1982

Dust

She tried teaching my relatives' daughter piano but gave up after two weeks. She remarked contemptuously: "I'm not used to getting money for nothing, but she hasn't got even a hint of talent."

None of this means anything now. The girl was nevertheless forced to take piano lessons by the gloomy power of her parents' stubbornness. She's all grown up now and, as Pantofel had predicted, has chosen a different career for herself. Finally, those years, endless and indistinguishable from one another, are long behind us. They broke us, aged us, tested us, at times imperceptibly, but always cruelly.

We lived in the same building: our family on the fifth floor, hers on the first. Why did I invite myself over to her place one time and then began to come over, if not often, certainly regularly? She was old enough to be my mother. We didn't have any shared interests. Moreover, she would greet me rather coldly, never seeming happy to see me.

At first it seemed to me that I would hang out with Pantofel for the sharpness of her tongue, her merciless criticism of everyone and everything. However, there was a different reason: in the tone of her speech, in her gestures, in the air of her little apartment I subconsciously, yet clearly noticed the heavy breathing of fate itself.

"Yes, I'm listening. Oh, it's you..." Pantofel would mutter into the receiver, clearly disgruntled, but would invariably invite me over.

Only now have I come to understand the feelings that came over her like a heavy fog. She was happy to see me, even though she continued to speak to me with a smirk on her face, spitting her words out through her teeth. Of course, she was happy to see me: finally, she had the opportunity to say all her secret thoughts out loud, without hiding. These were the thoughts she didn't feel dignified sharing with her gentile friends.

"Jews are dust," Pantofel would repeat as a provocation.

She was sure that her claims needed no justification, but sometimes she was in the mood to expand on her metaphor:

"...haven't you ever wondered *why* they are so hated everywhere they go? You see, it's not so simple. A people, like any person, has forty lives and has to die off at the right time, get out of the way for younger peoples. But Jews... They have long overstayed their welcome and now are just getting in everyone's way: they keep on cheating, adapting, getting involved wherever possible... well, everyone is tired of their eternal sorrow, their claims to omniscience and powers of foresight: all this has already happened, it's happened already... And man wants to get everywhere with his own mind! It's why we despise those old men in our lives that constantly try to warn us, to teach us something. You know of course that the Japanese would take their own old farts out into the mountains, straight to their graveyards before they got too annoying— and when the time comes, they just die there. That's the way to do it!"

Sometimes she would interrupt her own monologue by energetically flinging her hand—as if everything were already obvious and clear: "dust, only dust..."

She'd sit in front of me like an old ballerina unable to relax on her armchair out of habit. Pantofel's pose accurately reflected the essence of her strange existence. I sometimes wondered why she lived as if out of all the feelings that had clawed at and troubled her only intense hatred was left—her hatred for her own people that paradoxically seemed to keep her warm.

I remember one time an incredulous Pantotel directed a question at me, a question she had clearly posed to herself many times:

"Dust... really, what is dust? Why does it come into existence around where humans live? Haven't you notice that a recently vacated room has barely any dust?"

I suspect no one had any clue what hidden thoughts and feelings Klara Pantofel kept wound in a tight coil of silence. At the music school, where she had been the head teacher for many years until retirement, they had definitely noticed: Pantofel was particularly strict towards students and teachers who were Jewish. She never looked for flaws in them, but never forgave them for whatever flaws they showed either. They had all assumed that this was a typical feverishly Jewish provision: what if others accuse you of showing favoritism to "your own?"

But I was sure that Klara Pantofel no longer harbored any fears on that account, or any account for that matter.

In remembering her, I suddenly notice that I unwittingly avoid describing anything to do with her. For example, describing her one-bedroom apartment, where everything looked like a provincial hospital—everything was clean, but faceless; describing her clothes—similarly lacking in personality; or how she would constantly pour me green tea: "It's healthy!"

Now my mind turns to something else. Anti-Semitism among Jews themselves is not as mysterious as one would assume. It's a counterintuitive, but very understandable reaction from a person who's been chased down by fate. Sometimes you start to hate your own tribe, who are allegedly to blame for all your bad luck and unhappiness. Sometimes, in a strangely abstract turn, you can't stand yourself.

At the heart of Klara Platofel's anti-Semitism was a kind of despair—the despair of multiple generations collected in the soul of a person.

She never complained about anything. I only learned about the fates of her family members after many long conversations, completely by accident I would say. During the revolution, her grandfather was trampled in the Kishenev pogrom[4]. Her mother and father were taken to the camps as enemies of the people in 1937 (at the time, Klara was working in Siberia after finishing conservatory).

Why didn't she get married? No one ever asked her, though even in my memories she was quite attractive. But it was impossible to imagine anyone standing beside Pantofel: all of her being emanated an off-putting energy that incinerated any normal person.

So, her theory about Jews, not at all original, grew slowly in her lonely thoughts. The world was perfectly just, she reasoned, so if life itself forces Jews out, that means that they have no choice but to leave.

So, who did she had in her life?

I knew that sometimes her former student would come to visit — an eternally melancholy old maid; the young woman thought it was her "duty to help" her old teacher, but Pantofel would just bitterly make fun of her sorrows.

Once, during the summer, I met Klara Mikhailovna's sister, who had survived both the camps and the war. From evacuation she returned to Minsk, studied to be an engineer, got herself an alcoholic husband and a son, but only traveling around the world brought her any joy in life.

Klara Pantofel remained a fragile teenager all her life, but her sister turned out to be a hardy brunette through and through. She told me all about her travels, her eyes sparkling, and showed me her notebook, where she had meticulously copied out all her routes. She spoke the way people talk about love, blissfully unaware of the banality of what they are saying.

A year later, the "traveller" passed away from cancer. When she told me about it, Pantofel didn't shed a tear. She was mostly concerned about her nephew. He had just turned twenty-six. I don't remember where she said he worked, but I recall her mentioning he was taking night classes at university and was planning to get married.

"God forbid he marry a Jewish girl," Pantofel entreated in anguish, "I want my grandchildren to be happy."

After her sister's death, our meetings became more infrequent. I thought that her death must have completely convinced Klara of the truth of her life philosophy.

"I'm sorry, I'm busy," and the click echoed across the receiver.

One time I came over I instantly noticed something was different: it was as if she had shriveled up all of a sudden. And at the same time, fate was playing a joke on Pantofel — she looked more and more Jewish by the day. Her thin lips, always pursed, framed her deep wrinkled — the traces of a perpetual smirk. Her eyes — so-called "almond-shaped" — grew more sharply defined.

During our conversation, she mournfully looked at herself in the mirror, out of habit. I could tell that she was scared of the reflection. She despised her own face.

Perhaps that's why she stopped going outside.

When she died, Pantofel was buried hurriedly, the way all lonely people are buried.

When we returned from the graveyard, her building's superintendent was already waiting for her nephew: her apartment needed to be emptied as quickly as possible so that a single mother and her two children could take it. What about her things? Maybe they could be taken to the empty storage shed a few blocks away for the time being? Doubtful any of these considerations were made out of concern for the poor woman, more out of apprehension, they wouldn't want this Jewish nephew of hers to start some funny business and try to take the apartment himself.

A day later I happened to notice that the building janitor and some random guy (probably a friend of the new tenant) had carried all of Pantofel's belongings out of the house. They had piled everything at the entrance so that they could load it all into a truck later.

As it was turning around, the truck rode over the armchair the woman had loved to sit in. The chair burst into pieces, the springs uncoiled, pushing handfuls of dust from the furniture's dark innards.

A Theory

Their mystery drew me in back then, when the official biography was still incomplete. His typical Jewish eyes behind thick lenses.

Afterwards, after perestroika, strange details about his life began appearing, mostly in tabloid magazines, in the publications of "Russian patriots." Sometimes in respectable newspapers as well. As it turns out, his mother's surname was Fleckenstein. His father died young, probably was Jewish too.

Serious people didn't believe all that. Andropov[5] , really? Tell me: how could a Jew become the head of the KGB and later the leader of an anti-Semitic country? And all this during a time that a Jewish surname on your application was disqualifying. The reasoning was shaky. Take the mother, for instance, she was clearly just adopted by a Jewish family.

I myself was instantly convinced. I knew that prior to the revolution Jewish families couldn't adopt children they weren't related to. (That was the tradition—now's not the time to explain it further).

But that wasn't what convinced me. There were other details that stood out, lonely and cruel among the eulogies he received.

How carefully he hid the path that led to his childhood, boyhood, youth...

He left his first family in Yaroslavl and headed to work in Petrozavodsk, dreaming of a big career. Though not too long before, on the back of a family photo he had etched out a confession that reads like poetry:

"If you are ever lonesome, if you ever want to feel happiness even for a minute, look at this photograph and remember that in this world there exist two happy beings. Happiness is contagious. It enters our souls with the air we breathe, and a single moment can fix everything long years cannot."

What came into his soul later on? Where did he find happiness? He never saw his wife again. He only met his son and daughter as an old man, and not by his own choice.

The director of the orphanage where he grew up—they were so proud of him there—once had passed along his regards at a provincial party conference through a coworker. That coworker was foolish enough to deliver the warm words to their addressee and, subsequently, disappeared for a few years.

...Right now, I'm not thinking about the obvious cruelty that was predetermined by his office. I'm thinking about his cruelty towards himself. About his sleepless nights. About how he figured out his next move, always considering the possibility of being discovered. About how he would look at his photographs with suspicion.

Did he ever consider plastic surgery? Did he ever ask his doctors whether there were some special contact lenses that could change the look in his eyes?

2004

Aftertaste
of a Dream

"But why? Why do you need my dreams?" the old man's voice demands impatiently.

Then I ask myself: actually though, why?

* * *

Single sheets of paper, scraps—sometimes a few words scrawled on a receipt from the supermarket, from the doctor's office... Notes on dreams. Some things I have already forgotten, so I have to reread them a few times.

* * *

At one point, I had imagined this was going to be a huge archive with thousands of dreams.

Why then did I lose interest in the idea all of a sudden, twenty years after it had captured my imagination?

* * *

It turned out that not all dreams are special. On the contrary, so many are extraordinarily boring.

What interests me most now is the "aftertaste of a dream." This aftertaste appears when you are straining to remember your dream. And desperately trying to interpret its meaning.

Crows

On a snowy field right behind his home (where they were planning another five-story apartment building but never even started), he saw a flock of crows. At first, out of his usual pedantry he tried to count them, but failed. And that surprised him. The crows were cawing horribly, almost unbearable.

Then he woke up.

That summer morning, making his favorite sandwich for breakfast (bread, butter, cottage cheese and powidl fruit spread), he heard on the radio that there was war in the Middle East.

Then he was a corporate trust manager, calling himself "the useful Jew" almost seriously (actually though, he was never fired through the many company restructurings). He judged everyone and everything without reserve—all with a harsh cockiness that many found unpleasant.

He had a family back then, a wife and daughter. He had a strange nickname in his family—"communist." When I visited their home, I would hear his wife and daughter calling him: "Communist, come here!"

His wife died a long time ago, and his daughter moved up north for some unknown reason. Now he's an old man: when he meets people he doesn't know, he watches their faces with a terrified look in his eyes, quickly trying to hide the fact he is looking.

Some much of his life has been tossed aside as useless. But this dream of his—now a quarter of a century old—still remains in his being, troubling him to this day, scratching at the walls of his memory.

* * *

Telling me about this dream, B. himself draws a connection between it and the conflict in the Middle East. He thinks it might be a premonition. But then he's surprised again: why?

He's never been to Israel, never had any relatives there, and the country itself was nothing but a constant source of irritation for him.

One time at a meeting he spoke out against Zionism, his words curt but weighty. And he did so without any hints from his managers. And at home he told his loved ones—in the same creaky voice:

"...They're all just howling, chasing their ambitions, and then us over here, we get all the hate because of them."

How much genuine pain poured out and then evaporated in these words.

Awakening

She decides to tell me her dreams in a café. Earlier we had walked the wet little streets of the Lithuanian resort town of Druskininkai. It is late fall; the wind is raspy.

We walked into the café forty minutes before closing time. I carried ice cream and coffee from the bar (she said no to cake—"I'm on a diet").

And now we're sitting in front of one another. I notice that the shroud of silence is not too heavy for her to bear. She digs into the little white hill of her ice cream with her spoon. With the earnestness of a child, she savors its sweetness. Of course, it's this lack of pretension that makes her so charming.

Earlier that day she had confessed that only now, right before leaving for America can she be truly honest with another person. It's not that she was lying to everyone before, but she never gave anybody—anybody!—"any extraneous information" about herself.

She soon notices the patterns that emerge in my research into the dreams of Jews. I've taken note of them myself. Carefully sifting through the different dreams from her thirty years of life, she picks them off one by one. Then she stops to think. And sudden she says, the same child-like grin on her face:

"Can I tell you about... not quite a dream, no, but this one time I woke up? You know, I just realized that that one morning really affected me for the rest of my life. I got this rare sense of clarity—a clarity you only get right after a dream! And maybe then I'd be able to answer the most painful question of my existence. You're smiling? You're surprised? Oh, I'll surprise you alright—I was only seven years old!"

She's silent, then, as if double checking her memory:

"Well, yes, I'm right: it was 1965. Early morning in the summer. I woke up by myself, without an alarm clock. I was on summer break, so I didn't have to rush off to school. The room was filled with sunlight, and I looked over at our neighbors' house. Their windows were already opening up, I could hear a couple energetic voices coming from the street. My body felt light. By the way, I would frequently return to this feeling during yoga sessions... and then I thought: how great it is that I live in the Soviet Union! You're smiling again? But really, those were my exact thoughts. But then I instantly felt that something was getting in the way of the joy I felt, in the way of my bright tomorrow—as people liked to say back then. I concentrated really hard, and then I remember: I'm Jewish! Somewhere deep in my subconscious, probably, I came to decision: I need to overcome this!"

I don't ask her any questions. What if she falls silent again? But we're probably thinking the same thing—that all her subsequent life was precisely this sort of "overcoming."

I am thinking about her strange choices in life, and they all make sense now: she got married young to a Jewish man with a Russian surname who looked Slavic, studied Stanislavsky's method acting system for some reason, then got into yoga...

She looked at me, squinting a bit:

"My life has been a marathon, me running away from my childhood fears. And a marathon with a pointless goal: to overcome nature itself. But it's alright, it's alright... I'll come back to myself eventually. I'm still young, right?"

Her eyes are happy in the half-light, but it's still hard to see the future in them.

The Chase Motif

I'm waiting for recurring dreams. Oftentimes each ones contains a prophecy. But they are always a metaphor for someone's fate.

A typical story. One that repeats often. So often that I don't even bother recording it in full: only its new details and strange turns.

From twenty-five to thirty, I had only one dream that kept on repeating and repeating: I was being chased! And my pursuers weren't just threatening to beat me up—they were going to destroy me! I would recognize their faces instantly if I ever met them in real life. They were always the same faces. And I was always running away! I was saved only at the last moment, when it seemed like there was no hope left.

I never told anyone about these dreams of mine. But strangely enough, a friend of mine also had the same recurring dream... As you might have guessed, we had had a short fling and quickly moved, I'd say, into a happy friendship. At first, she didn't tell me anything about this shared dream of ours, but then one day made a confession out of the blue: "I'm scared for you!"

...in that dream the two of us walked into a restaurant in the evening. The restaurant was a small, poorly lit basement trying to seem hip and cool. We had just sat down and ordered, when all of a sudden, it seemed that my Jewish face had attracted the attention of the other customers. Someone said loudly: "They used to crucify your kind—back in the good old days!"

My friend was resourceful. She was able to divert the attention of our harassers with little jokes and coquetry, just long enough for us to escape.

We ran through side streets, hiding in building lobbies. Someone in the crowd chasing us had a knife in his hand.

It was a miracle we got away—like it always happens in dreams.

By the way, this friend of mine (she is Ukrainian) when we had just met told me condescendingly that Jews overexaggerate the extent of anti-Semitism, make up their oppression.

As a result, I never brought up this topic with her. In so doing, I felt awkward, like I was degrading myself. She, on the other hand, was too embarrassed, it seemed, to pity me.

Why did our dreams start twinning like that? What did they mean? I don't know. Everything was good in my life back then: I had my wife, my little boy, this friend beside me... we lived as one family. And it seemed that we were happy.

A Single Line

What nonsense people see in their dreams! Imagine: last night I dreamed about the letter I just received — the envelope it came in, more specifically. It hadn't been opened. It loomed before me, like up on a screen... What am I saying? That was it, I didn't see anything else. I started to read to carefully. A letter from Samarkand, from an acquaintance that I don't even write to that often. But the funny thing is that I instantly recognized her handwriting — her thick letters, one jumping away from the other on the page. And for some reason she added a note on the envelope itself — in the top corner, right above the address: "Does Dora love you?"

He falls silent. And then sharply inhales.

I search the pockets of his faded suede jacket — amid the keys and coins and caramel candies — looking for a medicine box. But, as always, he snaps out of it just in time.

It's been two months (spring 1986 — Yevsey Tseytlin) that we've been living together at the Writer's House in Golitsyno, a suburb of Moscow. I'll admit that I hadn't heard of him — either his Jewish surname or his Russian pseudonym — until recently. Not looking to become close friends with, I still learned quite a bit about him during this time: in the 30s, he wrote "production novellas," in the 40s and 50s he moved onto sketches about "heroes of the five-year-plan." Now — twenty years later —

he's silent, readying himself for memoirs. But it's obvious that he's spending his energy in vain, wasting it on vain conversation with old farts his age—on walks or in the TV room.

* * *

Some time I wait to make sure he won't have another episode. I get a profile view of his hairless scalp, his faded, tight lips, at once funny and deeply tragic.

I can't help but get to thinking about that odd, pointless single line on the top of the envelope he mentioned. Yes, sometimes, when they forget to mention some important piece of information in the letter itself, old folks and little kids add little notes like that. It's nonsense, really. But it truly seemed to grab him by the heart.

And Dora? That's his wife. As he described her, "the only bright spot in an ocean of falsity." She died six years ago.

At the Lake

We're walking along the lake. She's feeding bread to the swans.

"It's so nice here!" she says, greedily breathing in the air, "How nice..." And she lets a gray crumb drop into the water.

I fall back behind her. She notices and seemingly responds to herself after another "How nice":

"But if only I could stop having dreams."

I look at her, questioningly. She's stopped walking. Now she opens up a small foldable chair that she carries with her on walks. Her locks, dyed an unnaturally blonde, almost yellow, color, pop out from under the hood of her green camo jacket. She smiles at me with her little gray eyes. Around their edges I can see a net of red veins. Out of her huge bag, the size of a backpack, she takes out a pack of Prima cigarettes, lights up.

She is kind, even sentimental, but is really hard to talk to: she goes from being way too honest with everyone to whisper her responses to everyone under her breath.

I know what she used to be a journalist, even published a book of sketches. She never married, but retired early—due to her disability.

Dreams began tormenting her after the war. After returning from evacuation, still very young, she began collecting materials about the ghettos and concentration camps in the Baltic states—to honor the memory of her relatives who had perished.

* * *

What was so strange about these dreams? Or, perhaps, what was their consistent pattern?

The details that couldn't be mentioned in her sketches came to life in these dreams: back then these details were called "naturalistic particularities," the kind deemed unfit for mentioning in Soviet journalism.

Curiously, she often saw her own body, asleep, in her own dreams.

A few times she slept in one of those ghetto hideouts, the kind you could only access through the furnace. Around twenty people would cram themselves in there. Some would pass out or lose their minds from the lack of oxygen. That's why they'd check up on one another: from time to time someone would like a candle to illuminate their gray, half-dead faces. It was pure joy to fall asleep and no longer feel the demands of life on your shoulders.

And one time this joy visited her. She slept for a long time. She awoke from the crying of a nursing baby that her neighbor was holding in her arms. But soon the crying ceased. In the dark someone had thoughtlessly stuffed a pillow into the infant's face. Horrifyingly, no one protested this swift execution. The Germans were searching the hideout next door.

* * *

That was only a dream. But that sort of thing happened in these hideouts all the time—I've heard similar stores from ghetto prisoners once or twice. Why had this story, rehearsed in her dreams time and again, driven her to the hospital? Maybe it's the result of a writer's creative process? These thoroughly laid out plots, brightened by imagination but never written down don't let their authors live, sometimes literally...

She gets up. And now we start up slowly walking along the lake again.

She reads my mind:

"Don't worry, my dear, I've learned to manage this. The most important thing is to know yourself, know all your possible dreams, the times they strike you. The scariest ones get you from four to six in the morning. The heaviest thoughts also come around them. At one point I was scared of those hours, now I'm prepared—I wake before then, like I've set an alarm clock... I'll turn on the light, read a detective novel. Then I'll doze off again when the morning arrives. Those morning dreams are completely different: they're all warm and even. Haven't you noticed?

By the Way

Spring 1998—a meeting (at Yevgeny P's house) with a young American woman. Psychologist. For a while she was writing down the dreams of HIV positive individuals.

"Is there anything out of the ordinary in these dreams?"

"No, not really."

And then she shares a few of their plots with me:

"...A young man is driving fast on the highway. Suddenly, an automobile flies out and starts barreling down towards him. The other car is swiftly approaching. At the last moment, the young man manages to switch lanes. Thankfully, the lane over is nearly empty."

"...a woman is eating an apple. Suddenly she tastes a thin, sharp disk: her mouth fills with blood. Inside the apple she finds a razor blade. She barely manages to spit it out."

I instantly remember writing down something similar. The dreams of people who have found themselves at the very edge of life.

The Formula of a Dream

Long Walk to Forever. That's a title of a Kurt Vonnegut novel that, admittedly, has nothing to do with dreams.

Parisian Dreams

Our small hotel in the very center of Paris has a pompous sounding name: Grand Hotel. We reserved a room here a month ago on the recommendation of our friends in Chicago. And there really are very few surprises: it's relatively comfortable and clean. We don't need much else. My wife and I get back late, filled to the brim with Paris. And all we want to do is sleep (after watching the evening BBC news on the TV hung up from the ceiling).

There is one surprise though. But we've been well prepared for them: Isaac Babel[6] himself writes about how thin the walls are in a Parisian hotel. We can hear our neighbor's every word, nearly every little sound.

Right above us lives a Slovak family. They come back very late, right as we're falling asleep, and just start loudly laughing about something of their own, something we can't hear.

Nevertheless, I manage to have a dream with such an accompaniment. I wake up and then instantly doze off again. And the dream starts up again, right where it ended.

* * *

...I'm standing in a great hall, filled with people. Like everyone around me, I'm holding a pillow in my hands. Suddenly, we seem to receive the same invisible order and all take our pillows out of their cases and then proceed to shake their fluff into the center of the room. The pile grows to the point that the people in the center have to tamp it down.

And still the unruly feathers go flying upwards.

* * *

At night I instantly recognize the faces of some of the people standing in the hall.

There's my unageing "double." That's what I call this young man that looks so much like me. I bumped into him accidentally, a quarter of a century ago, at the Zheleznovodsk health center — in the bath pavilion.

A young Buryat, studying the habits of pigeons (we lived together in the dorm of the Moscow pedagogical institute: I was doing some sort of internship there, he was defending his PhD).

French Jews that my wife and I saw on our second day in the Marais quarter. They were walking quickly, wary for some reason. They walked in groups of three or four — as if they were supporting one another.

...But who gave the order to throw the fluff up in the air? If it had been Him, who had established, once and for all, the rhythm and meaning of human existence, then our deeds were as light as feathers. As the book of Ecclesiastes breathes out: "All is vanity and grasping for the wind."

Dancing on Ice

In the ghetto she lived in a dirty six-square-meter closet — together with her mother, two aunties, her married brother, and probably someone else too.

The same ritual repeated every evening. Newspapers were laid down in the corridor, followed by old sheets and a tiny pillow. She was seventeen. It took all her will to force herself not to notice the smells and sounds of the little room, filled to capacity with bodies.

She told me a dream of hers from that time in her life. "Did you have it often?" "I still see it now."

Here's the dream: nearly naked, lightly covered by something airy and white, she's racing on her skates on a huge icy arena...

I can hear the old self-doubt in her voice: she was never any good at dancing! Not to mention, she had never put on a pair of skates.

A dogmatic materialist, she would never stoop so low as to look into some petty little dream.

Still, they say that seeing yourself naked in a dream makes you experience the same feeling of shame as when you are awake. I don't know how she felt before but now, as a tall and thin older woman, she hasn't felt even the slightest awkwardness in a long time. She bosses everything and everyone around — her neighbors, the families of her son and daughter.

But no! There are times when the old woman isn't so sure of herself. Early in the morning she quietly slinks to the bathroom with a little bundle in hand. Everyone's still asleep, she thinks. She would surely be made incredibly uncomfortable if she'd ever find out that through the slightly open door her twelve-year-old grandson, having just woken up on the couch, is watching her. He can easily see how his grandmother comes into the bathroom, how she takes out a shaving brush and razor from her bundle, how she squints nearsightedly at the mirror while lathering herself with shaving cream. And then she shaves her not yet flabby cheeks...

The boy gloomily stares into the ceiling. In the meanwhile, after rubbing aftershave on her face, she puts on a thick layer of foundation and walks out into the world — completely born anew, triumphant.

A Philological Story

One time my friend was teaching at a university, researching Russian literature of the 20s. I'm just setting the scene so you get the picture.

I get a call from him in early August.

"...you know what I saw in my dreams last night? A rowdy literary meeting. I myself spoke up during the meeting — I asked one very important literary mister a question. I didn't recognize him when I was asking him a question. Then I asked him, and it turned out it was Yakov Elsberg[7] !"

My friend falls silent. He's taking pleasure in my amazement. I instantly recall the biography and bibliography of this Yakov Elsberg. A famous literary scholar and critic in his time. Like many Soviet Jews, he had a very keen sense of the *current moment* and what it demanded of him. He wrote articles about Futurism and Gorki, Herzen and Saltykov-Schedrin, very intelligently, but with a distinctive hint of vulgar sociologism... We can forgive this vulgar sociologism if we examine Elsberg's work objectively, if we remember the times when they were written. Moreover, it was scholarship that was his life's main work.

As a result of his denunciations, there were many young graduate students, famous scholars and writers that were sent to the camps...

Who forced him to do it? The operations of these state apparatuses are well-known, but we can gather more information about Elsberg's case specifically from the title of his 1924 volume: "From the inner prison of the State Political Directorate (the notes of an inmate)."

In these cases, all questions are always rhetorical. But still: "What did you ask him?" I ask my friend about his dream.

"I was just curious if he had a good memory."

In his dream he didn't hear the response. So, he soon returned to the same dream, looking for the answer.

Meeting

Thoughts and images as they appear in dreams have their own logic, of course. But what is it exactly? For example, when I see my father in my dreams, I instantly remember that he has been gone a long time. But, at the same time, I can never remember that he died already and I was the one who buried him.

It always seems to me as if he has merely driven off somewhere for a long time. As if he had just dropped off the face of the earth.

My father appears in my dreams quietly, almost imperceptibly. He's calm, but stern and unsmiling. Typically, he sits a bit to the side of everyone, looking around and listening in. Always silent.

In one of these dreams, one of the more recent ones, it's all different.

I catch sight of my father as he walks into the room. I walk towards him. We embrace one another for a long time, our eyes welling up with tears we're trying to hide.

Typically, my father doesn't wear a tie (only rarely, for "special occasions," and only one of those pre-tied ties). His top two buttons are always unbuttoned. I'm looking at him very intently now, at his sun-burnt, freckled, and wrinkled neck and reddish gray hair on his chest. But, look, what are those big cuts on his chest? They're roughly sewn up, barely healed — covered over by a band-aid.

So, I get to thinking: cuts like that appear on the body after a pathologist's autopsy. But we had decided not to do one! We had just buried him as he was.

Dream logic is incomprehensible, yet stubborn. Even after thinking about my father's death, I don't see his dead body. But then — one time — I walk over to his grave.

Here's the cemetery. Atop a hillock roasted in the sun near the Kyrgyz town of Jalal-Abad. Rough, prickly grass all around. The former little poplar tree over the course of thirty years has grown to define this view, managing to engulf almost all of the area inside the metal fence.

Below the poplar stands a bench. Only there's no one left to sit on it. We had spent a long time choosing the spot. We were looking for a plot that wouldn't get flooded by the rare, yet heavy rainstorms.

Then we tried not to think about the fact that my father, coming here all the way from Siberia, never felt at home in Central Asia. Of course, he hadn't wanted to stay here forever, amid these sandy hills.

Brother

I got very sick that year. It is traditional for Jews to get a new name when that happens. This isn't just a Jewish custom, by the way. It is an ancient wisdom, an attempt to change what fate has in store for you...

Once I got a new name myself (to be more precise, a new name got added to my old, familiar name). I won't go into details about this ritual. I merely want to recall a dream that I had three nights in a row around that time. Perhaps it was prophetic?

* * *

...at the entrance to my apartment I suddenly encounter my father. Standing next to him is a man lost in thought, who bears a strong resemblance to me. Truly all three of us look alike — my father, this stranger, and me. And we are all the same age — all around sixty.

"This is your brother, my son. Love him," my father says with an unusual softness in his voice.

I am at a loss for words: I've never had a brother.

My father, however, isn't waiting for an answer. Together we walk into the apartment. For some reason I notice how strangely the door closed behind us — slowly, not all at once, but leaving no way out for us.

* * *

I had this dream soon after my doctor dryly yet calmly pronounced the name of a disease I had never heard of before.

I told my wife and mom about this dream, something I don't normally do. Too often the dream vanishes when you try to retell it.

Neither of them made much of the dream. It was half a year later that I sudden understood its alarming and slippery meaning. I was my own "brother" — a man with a new name and a new fate stretching out in front of me.

The Origin of Night Terrors

These past few years I read everything there was to read about dreams. From Freud and Jung to Borges and Castaneda, from eastern mystics to a variety of dream interpreters. Of course, I asked the question: what does Judaism have to say on the matter?

Moysha B is one of my fellow travellers in looking for an answer. How long have we known each other? Probably almost fourteen years.

Six years before we met, he had left his entire left back in Russia, including himself, a typical member of the Moscow intelligentsia. In America, the old Misha became the new Moysha, part of the Lubavitch Hasidic community. A programming job and a small well-decorated two-story house don't prevent Moysha and his wife Liba to live the way people of their faith did at least a century ago. They live in the warm world of Hassidic traditions, in a firm and simple aim to do good, in a constant anticipation of the Messiah's coming.

"Where do we go at night when we follow the path of our dream?" Moysha repeats his question, "Probably, we don't go very far."

In the *Kitzur Shulchan Aruch*[8], where the laws of a Jewish way of life are laid out concisely, we read: "...while we sleep, our immortal soul leaves the body, and it ends up under the sway of unclean forces..."

"That's why when we wake up, we must wash our hands as soon as possible—we bear the trace of death on our fingers."

"According to the Kabballah, they who do not wash their hands after sleep and walk the distance of four forearms [about two meters], put their soul in grave danger."

And that is the origin of night terrors.

Someone Remembers

If you really think about it, dreams are similar to our past lives.

L. B. tells the story:

"In Austro-Hungary, back in the old days, two Jewish families, living in two different cities, decided to marry into one another. They had never met before. They set everything up like they were supposed to, with matchmakers (badchens) and everything. The groom was supposed to arrive a week before the wedding, but got caught up and got there a few hours before the chuppah. Predictably, the bride was worried, desperately staring out the window. At last, she caught sight of the groom—and burst into tears: "I won't marry him..."

When he came into the house, the groom grasped the situation instantly: "I must speak with the bride this instant..." Ten minutes after their conversation, the bride was joyous and ready to stand under the chuppah. What changed?

The groom had a hunchback. More specifically, his back had two humps. So, what did he tell his bride that made her calm down and get excited? "When heaven decided who would become my wife, I saw that the girl I was to marry would have a hunchback. I knew that I was destined to have a hunchback as well, so I started bargaining about my bride-to-be: couldn't I just have two humps instead?"

And the most interesting part of L. B.'s story? The groom (a wiseman from a famous Jewish family) wasn't trying to mollify his bride. She suddenly remembered it all herself, like it was a dream she had seen a long time ago: and everything happened just like that.

"Very Boring Sex"

In my dreams, night after night, I would see an enormous bed: this sort of fabulous "sex stadium." But everything that happened in my dreams would inevitably disappoint me. You won't believe me, but, in reality, everything was quite different! I had just turned thirty and girls, like cards in an infinite deck, swapped themselves out for one another in my bedroom.

The most paradoxical thing was that I didn't really think of this as youth's typical lasciviousness. I always kept the most important thing in mind. I really wanted to get married, earnestly sought to find my own spot in bed... And never managed to find it. Then I got married after all, losing my patience and my mind in the process. After about three months I came to a common realization, one that struck so many around me—the person I was sharing a bed with was a stranger to me. But my wife at the time was pregnant. We separated two years later, when my daughter had grown up a bit.

And the same thing started up again. The same deck of cards, one loaded with only queens. But I wasn't looking for anyone anymore. I kept on having the same dreams—a huge bed and very boring sex.

* * *

He had blue eyes, full anguish and still piercing. A kind of endless charm and charisma. We are sitting in a big apartment in the center of Vilnius. He got it from his parents when they left for Israel. He had worked as a factory legal adviser, now (in the mid-90s) he is an unlucky salesman.

Oh, Mark, Mark! Where are you and who are you with?

Red Currant

How do I write down other people's dreams? I ask around inconspicuously, "by the way." I don't want to hear any external inventions or fantasies: the very genre of the dream presupposes them.

I want to avoid unnecessary theorizing.

I also understand that the desire to edit one's dream is strong.

In my dreams I've visited the West many times. Last night, something mysterious happens... I walk over to make a call at the inter-city phone booth by the post office. And I get attacked... I get the sense he knew I was coming, was expecting me. What do I do? I forcefully push away my assailant. He falls to the ground and doesn't get up. I lean over and look down in horror: is he dead?

Yes! When he fell, this stranger split his head, part of his skull even went flying off to the side... I never thought I had it in me to strike with such force. It is odd, though, that there doesn't seem to be any blood anywhere. Upon closer inspection, it turns out his head was made of plastic. This was no human. This was a robot.

* * *

He is from Kyiv. "Semyon... I'm part of an organization," he tells me, modestly. He is grey, portly, rosy-cheeked. He's wearing jean shorts and a white T-shirt.

In the early 90s we stand together in line at the market — waiting to buy some red currant. My dog, a black poodle named Count, starts licking Semyon's hairy ankles all of a sudden. We exchange a few phrases as we walk to the bazar. It's stuffy out. Our conversation is languid. Then suddenly he says to me: "So I saw this dream last night..."

Maybe the red currant we were waiting for reminded Semyon of the blood he was looking for but couldn't find in his dream?

Leprosy

They are all naked. They're lying side by side — young men and women. A small island, shores washed by the ocean. Sand so wondrous, so yellow, sand as soft as flour.

Why don't they seem to be bothered by being naked and being surrounded by so many other naked people?

This normally happens in a moment of mortal peril. The body's voice tends to fall silent.

* * *

...Yes, we only seem to think about the little wounds that now and then appear on our bodies.

For some reason I know the exact name of this illness — "leprosy."

Each of us has a little tube of cream in their hands. Sometimes the wounds seem to be healing. But then they open up again, suddenly growing bigger...

It's curious: we never seem to consider other dangers. This disease isn't the only threat we face! This small island is shrinking before our eyes — nothing can stop the ocean slowly engulfing it. Death is unavoidable no matter what we do.

* * *

This dream seems difficult to decipher, no? Only at first glance. In the Torah (specifically in the Tazria) this special disease is well-documented as punishment for one of the gravest sins of Judaism — slander.

I'll clarify one thing: leprosy back then had nothing to do with the illness that nowadays gets treated in leper colonies.

All That Came True

I'm eleven years old. A big Siberian city, where the asphalt becomes soft in the summer heat. A city that the newspapers call "garden city" for some reason. My school is an old two-story building with carved platbands. There are only two Jewish students in my grade: G. F. (a smart, calm girl with gray eyes and long braids) and me.

Naturally, I'm the one teased for being Jewish.

I keep this from my parents for a long time. First of all, I'm embarrassed for some reason. Second of all, they're not wrong: I really am Jewish.

Finally, I decide to tell them. Mom and dad confer with one another all evening. The next day they head over to my homeroom teacher. And not to her office at school, mind you—to her house. I follow them over timidly—probably so that I can offer my testimony.

The teacher greats us with a sluggish hospitality, but also with complete understanding:

"This is unacceptable!"

Then she sighs:

"But what can I do? I'm Jewish too..."

The teacher is about forty years old. Her face is waxy yellow. Her husband is an officer. Her two daughters go to our school—quietly, not making a big deal. This homeroom teacher of mine doesn't look Jewish at all.

I'm telling you all of this to give a sense of my childhood atmosphere—the *prehistory* of my dream, so to speak.

* * *

I see myself in my own dream, where nothing seems to be happening. Before me I see a photograph that seems to be moving... in it I'm thirty years old. I'm wearing a red sheepskin jacket. I'm talking to someone of a small flip phone. What's more, I can somehow tell that I'm definitely in America.

* * *

This dream has stayed in my memory my whole life. It comes into my mind from time to time (sometimes with shock, sometimes with a slight grin). But I've never shared it with anyone. But I couldn't help myself just now. Maybe because this dream has come true?

Well, I did come to America when I was forty-seven. However, everything else happened exactly like I saw it. Down to the sheepskin coat that my mom gave me as a gift right after I moved. Down to the flip phone I had just used to call my daughter.

Honey

For forty long years she couldn't rid herself of this dream. Then I heard recently: as she lay dying, slowly losing consciousness, she was moaning out:

"Honey's... sweet... to drink..."

At first this dream seemed typical to her. One of a thousand mindless dreams that any one of us sees over the course of their life.

This dream was always remembered crystal clear—all the way down to the minor details, down to the spittle in her throat: someone was slowly pouring honey from a large three-liter jar into tiny little bottles.

She had this dream regularly: after dropping off for a couple months, it would reappear with those exact same details. The honey glowed through the glass of the jar: it had barely managed to thicken, still quite liquid. You want to drink it all up, to press your mouth to its rim! A slice of white bread would be the perfect side dish.

For several years she was sure: this dream was the aftereffect of starvation—she had lived through the Leningrad blockade![9] However, in 1948 a gypsy told her, as if it were common knowledge, that in dreams honey typically points to some sort of pleasure. At first, she believed the gypsy, but then, remembering day after bitter day of the blockade, burst out in hysterical laughter: oh really, pleasure?!

She thought she had at last understood the meaning of the dream in 1956 when she met Fira Kagan at a Moscow pastry shop on Gorky Street. During the war, Fira had managed to climb out of a hole where her entire shtetl had been buried.

"...Fira told me that her sister Rivka had died. We were twins; before she was shot, that means, she had just turned nineteen. We both had this animalistic desire to survive. During the blockade, I scavenged for food all over—wherever I could find it, just following what my instinct told me:

where, who from, when. And we never got caught! Right before she died, Rivka threw all her clothes into the collective pile and crawled around naked on all fours — grabbing the boots of the polizei... of course, they showed her no mercy!"

So, if you count from the mid 50s, she had half her life ahead of her. "The sweet half," she told me confidently.

In my opinion, her interpretation was too straightforward.

She always loved to extemporize, never letting anyone get a word in the middle of her monologues. Throwing them off life like a dry shell, I'm trying to figure out the most important thing. She moved across the country eight times. She had a bright lineup of husbands and lovers who were all strangely difficult to distinguish from one another. Finally, there was the tumor, discovered far too late of course in Tashkent.

Was that really it? I must have forgotten something.

* * *

She told me about her dream soon after meeting me. And she added, as if anticipating my question: "No, I've never had diabetes."

She was one of my distant relatives — so distant that now perhaps I would not be able to explain exactly how we were related. I met her by accident, around two years before she died. She had already retired. She had previously worked as a hairdresser in different cities, towns, villages. I instantly appreciated how fearless she was: she wasn't afraid of moving, of parting ways with people sharply and forever. This wasn't just my first random impression. Afterwards she didn't even get scared of her malignant tumor — she got a clear diagnosis from her doctors, understood that the tumor had already metastasized, and underwent a difficult, unnecessary operation. With the same calmness she traded her apartment (from a bigger to a smaller square footage, getting back an additional payment) and sold nearly all her furniture. She bequeathed a considerable sum of money to a married couple. They were a quiet pair who she had found to take care of her when she got sick. They had promised to visit her grave.

Her lonely and fearless death made sense to me. But still, the question remains: what was her life? All those long years—what did it symbolize—this seemingly simple dream of hers?

Esther's Secrets

"There's nothing peculiar here," Esther says, "Of course, you can measure out your life in dreams."

We're drinking coffee in her small kitchen. She lives in a large-paneled apartment complex near the Kalvariju Market in Vilnius.

She's chain-smoking cigarettes as she tells me about her dreams.

Esther's dreams are like poems—their surprising associative links have the same undeniable weight. Lest you forget, you must write dreams down right away. But I only wrote down one of Esther's dreams—completely by accident, on a random scrap of paper. A dream about how she taught the editor-in-chief of the party magazine "Soviet Lithuania."

This dream suddenly connected all the different poles of her life for me.

Esther worked as an editor for "Soviet Lithuania" for a number of decades. During perestroika she remember the Hebrew she had learned in childhood and began teach it to adults, mostly those that were moving to Israel for "permanent residence."

"If I'm not mistaken..." she says, taking a drag from her cigarette and hiding the stark bareness of her confession in a cloud of smoke, "...If I'm not mistaken, those were the happiest years of my life."

A few months ago, Regina K introduced the two of us. She had studied with Esther and, with her habit of always doing something special for her acquaintances, she suddenly decides to throw a party for her classmates. She invites me to join.

After that, now and then, Esther and I exchange calls. And after that we (rarely) take walks together in the evening. And after that we drink coffee or tea in the kitchen.

Our age gap—about forty years—only strengthens our friendship.

She divulges to me the "secrets" of her life—Esther used that word herself, ironically.

More than anything she loves telling me her dreams.

The dreams of her youth are filled to the brim with music (Esther was studying at a conservatory back then).

Dreams from the era of "fight against rootless cosmopolitanism." The main characters of these dreams are Esther herself and her friends. Most of them are no longer with us, though the fears from that time are alive and well.

Dreams about "love long ago" always come up unexpectedly. Esther's sweetheart was the wondrous Russian prose writer K. V[10]. The Soviets squeezed him out of Russia, but that's how he and Esther met one another—at the editorial office of "Soviet Lithuania."

Colorless dreams of her current loneliness.

Dreams in color, imported from Israel, where she improved her Hebrew by taking classes.

"Warm dreams" connected with her trips to Finland, where her son works as a doctor.

I don't write down Esther's dreams. Once she asks me to never tell anyone the "secrets" she's shared with me. And it seems to me that writing down her dreams, even for myself, is a betrayal of her friendship.

After my departure for Chicago, I see Esther two more times.

Her letter is typed on an old typewriter. Some of the letters are barely visible and circled with a shaky pen. She wishes me luck in America, but there's an unstated message in the letter: Esther wants to make sure to say goodbye.

It's easy to recognize her on the pages of K. B.'s novel *Here Came the Giant*, reprinted in 2002. It's clearly their love story. The novel was written more than thirty years ago, but Esther seems so alive here: as beautiful as her namesake-queen, brave and paralyzed by fear all at once that she can't bring herself to admit to anyone. It's not surprising that it's easier for her to tell me her dreams.

And again, now I am deep in thought, having just learned about Esther's death from the abovementioned Regina K: you really can measure out your life in dreams.

Not in years, not in wrinkles, not in loves that pass like an illness — only in dreams.

From childhood to old age.

These dreams will rustle. Delight. Alarm. Force you to think long and hard. Then, at last, disappear.

And that's a person's path for you.

Not remembering
it all

Death on the Life Line

Jewish wisdom has claimed time and again that the face reflects a person's essence. This idea, now commonplace, isn't that simple. Many times, throughout my life I have met people that have bravely compared their external appearance to their internal experience of themselves, only to painfully find a lack of correspondence. Or they would helplessly run away from their own face.

...Seven years ago in Chicago, at a local bookstore, a beautiful older woman said hello to me. She realized that I didn't recognize her:

"My name is Lea... Remember: early 70s, Kemerova... at the library..."

I instantly remembered her, as if lightning had flashed before my eyes, clearing up my dusty pictures of the past. You don't meet that many Jews in Siberia. That's why they're so sharply distinct in a crowd of faces — either as precious gems or as caricatures of themselves (if they're worn out by their endless fears). This woman from the library wasn't that attractive physically, but there was something magnetic about her. At the same time, I felt a strange, terrifying coldness emanating from her.

Expecting to hear a bitter tale of Jewish life, I tried to get to know her better on many occasions. But we would only greet one another politely, with a certain weight and significance. Then I left Siberia for good.

"...I've heard a lot about you, I've bought your books. If you want, I can tell you about myself," she suggested all of a sudden, "Not now, of course. If it's convenient, I could come to your office one of these days. My husband and I are in Chicago for the week, visiting some friends."

And she really came. It was a gloomy February morning. It was sleeting—the thorny pellets were the seeds of a frozen over, angry snow. But the woman's face was calm and bright. She smiled mysteriously at me—just as she had back in Siberia. Only now there was no coldness about her at all.

"Glad you came... May I hang your coat up?"

With a light and natural movement, she handed me her fur coat, sat in the chair, and accepted a cup of coffee. She began her confession without introduction—as if she had sensed my particular interest in her all those years ago. So, I wrote her story down, trying to be as faithful as possible.

* * *

...Don't be embarrassed for not recognizing me right away. That's not surprising. Back then, when we were in Siberia together, I was different—a fragile thirteen-year-old brunette. Now, I'm a blonde. And I'm sixty... oh, no need to comfort me. I'm not at all ashamed of my age. On the contrary. I can explain why.

Back then, I wasn't naturally so small and fragile—I had this vague, but uncompromising feeling that my body was somehow inappropriate. It was easy for me to forget to eat. It seemed that I didn't need food at all. I had bad posture even before my teenage years, trying to hide my breasts from onlookers' eyes. When I got older, I started dressing fashionably, I suppose, but the dresses I chose were always dull, no bright colors, and a size too big—the dresses were also a way of hiding. The only thing I couldn't hide was my face. That was the only thing that exposed me, you could say. Whenever I'd happen upon a mirror, it was as if I saw my body from outside myself: those big eyes, frozen in fear, that soft skin, that thick, black hair with nervous curls.

I worked in the section of the library, where new books are processes and readers never come around, so I didn't talk to too many people at work. And I was happy with that set-up. People at the library said that they loved me. But I would describe their feelings towards me as benevolent indifference. Benevolent because they could tell that I was never selfish or jealous.

They were the ones who should have been jealous of me, but they would have thought to be just looking at me. I had a husband, a successful designer. Moreover, he was tall and charming. He had this thick mustache, the color of wheat. We had a daughter—like her father she was trying to have it all, doing school and a competitive sports program—and also managing to cook at home. We were living in a three-bedroom co-op apartment.

Nobody understood my eternal melancholy. But they got used to it eventually.

Even though we had little in common, my husband and I strangely got along back then. I never asked him for anything. I never demanded that he hand his paycheck over to me, never forbade him from going out drinking with his buddies. Maybe that was why he only drank on special occasions and very responsibly, about twice a month, why he'd put his money in a cookie tin that sat in a kitchen cabinet.

We're all adults here, so you'll excuse my honesty: every night our lovemaking was the same as it was on our wedding night: he always seemed to be a bit surprised. Once he said as much himself: "We've lived together for twelve years, but I feel like I still haven't discovered all of you yet." He faintly sensed some secret I was keeping from him, some words left unsaid. Of course, he couldn't express this sensation out loud: after all, what sort of secrets could I be hiding from him, the first and only man I had ever slept with?

But there was a secret: I knew that I was going to die at thirty-five.

...A fortuneteller told me so.

At the time I was studying in Leningrad, at the institute of culture.

It was the end of the semester, and my friend and I were hurrying off to an exam. A gypsy woman stopped us on our way with that age-old question:

"Tell me, my dears, what time is it?"

I knew that this was the typical way of doing things for street fortunetellers: strike up a conversation, then sweettalk their "targets" into giving their money away. But I still looked at my watch:

"1:15."

The gypsy woman got even closer, speeding through her spiel with great confidence:

"My lovelies, shall I do a reading for you? Tell you the whole truth?"

My friend jumped away:

"No, we don't need that... we already know everything we need to know."

But I, fully transfixed, let the old woman take me by the hand.

"Let's go, let's go, my lovely..."

The fortuneteller led me beyond the corner of a pinkish six-story building. Corpulent and lively, she and her hard and raspy voice seemed to be ageless — she could have been anywhere between fifty and seventy.

At first all of her movements were mechanical and learned, like she wasn't putting a lot of thought into her words and gestures. She took my hand — her hand, coarse and warm, was covered in rings. Unfolding my palm, she brought it closer to her eyes:

"I'll tell you the whole truth..."

And then she fell silent. And I stood there, with a neutral expression on my face — in part so that I didn't embarrass myself in front of passersby, in part so that I didn't offend the fortuneteller. I was calmly looking at the drops of sweat that were hanging off the gypsy woman's chin, in little gray chin hairs.

"The whole truth" came out suddenly:

"You've had a great tragedy, my dear... a great tragedy... everyone from your roots has ditched you."

That's exactly the expression she used — "ditched you." She raised her heavy lids and looked me right in the eye: presumably, she was looking in them to find something to comfort me with.

"You're going to have a husband, a child..."

She fell silent, the whites of her eyes flashing:

"Where did your family die?"

I named a regional center in Belarus...

"I know it," the fortuneteller nodded. She might have actually been to the place: gypsies end up everywhere in their travels. Again, the woman stared at my palm intensely. Finally, she said:

"Well, I will tell you the whole story, my girl. Your fate was to die with them, but then your fate was delayed. There it is, you see, your death—at thirty-five. I don't usually tell this kind of truth... but I've taken pity on you... take care... take care of everything that you've got left."

She took the five rubles that I instinctively took out of my bag (a substantial amount of money for me back then), stuck the banknote somewhere into the frills of her flowery skirt and sighed:

"My girl, we also got threatened by gun and fire..."

When I caught up with my friend, she laughed:

"So, when's the wedding gonna be?"

I continued the joke: "My fiancé awaits."

I was out of it the rest of the day. But everyone assumed that I was just nervous before the exam. But that day I still hadn't let the words of fortuneteller's prophecy really sink in, didn't let myself believe in her exact predictions about my time of death.

After the exam, I headed to the movie theater with my friend to watch *Spring on Zarechnaya Street*[11] a second time. At the dorms I wolfed down halva with my tea. But that night I couldn't fall asleep. It wasn't even the prophecy that was so antithetical to my young, twenty-year-old body that was still so full of yearning for life. The gypsy woman had expressed that which I had long known and felt deep down: that my existing was somehow unfair. Unfair to my parents, to my little sister, to my grandmother—all of them dead.

...And I was shy before that, anti-social even. Now, coming home from the institute, I would get into bed, turn to the wall, and stare it—as if trying to look through it.

"My head hurts!"—that was the excuse I'd give my girlfriends, so that they wouldn't bother me with questions.

Those days I tried to travel back to my hometown many times. But it never worked. A thick screen covered up the life I had left behind forever. I should imagine them based on what my aunt had told me. But only the most general sketches. No specific details.

My father worked as the director of a print shop. We lived right by that print shop. In an annex with three tiny rooms. in the first room lived my parents; in the second—my grandmother with the one-and-a-half-year-old Bertochka; in the third—me and my older sister Bella.

I still remember the stretch of street, the yard, two benches, where workers sat on their smoke breaks, and the quite distinctive smell of print shop ink.

I was only three when in early May of 1941 I was sent to Novosibirsk to stay with extended family—my mother's sister, also named Lea. My aunt was unmarried and in every single letter begged my parents to send me over to stay with her—just for a bit, just for the summer.

I never saw my hometown again. I had no place to return to. And I hadn't the strength. After the war, through letters to our former neighbors, my aunt and I learned what kind of death befell each of my family members. My father died fighting in a guerilla squadron. And my mom, my grandmother, and my sister were all shot in late fall of 1941.

...My shock from the prophecy last two weeks. Then it went away. I stopped spending all day lying in bed—and returned to my life from before.

You know, all of a sudden I got prettier. Lost weight, my eyes were still full of sorrow, but my facial features started feeling more defined and complete: this typically happens to women ten-fifteen years older than me.

It was as if I really started living in place of my loved ones. The signs of this vicarious life were subtle. Bella, my older sister, loved the ballet (even though she had only ever seen two performances with our parents in Leningrad). And that fall I started frequenting the Mariisnky[12], acquiring tickets by any means necessary.

Bertochka, my younger sister, was ready to give everything in the world up for pastille candies. Even when she got sick, she would happily drink any concoction given to her once she had received a pocketful of those candies. That detail accidentally lodged itself in mind and stayed with me through the years. I preferred those cheap pastille candies to all others.

People once again became drawn to me. Young men—there weren't that many in my major—tried to catch my attention, asked me out to the movies or to dances. Girls told me their secrets, asked for my advice if they were sewing something: "You've got the best taste, Lea." Some of these people, like my husband after them, sensed that I held a secret inside me. It was akin to sensing another person's death nearby or some still unclear danger up ahead. And secrets attract people—we all love to figure them out.

I really liked many things about Valera, as a matter of fact. First and foremost, he had all those qualities I lacked. I was drawn to his victorious, happy confidence—in him and in life itself. That feature seemed to hypnotize others as well. And that's why everything worked out for him. By the way, if my husband were different—all spiritually confused, unsure of himself, vulnerable to fate and those around him—I probably would have told him my "whole truth" sooner or later.

...My life seemed to go on without me. After I finished college, we moved to Kuzbass. Soon our daughter was born. Two years later my aunt suddenly passed away from a stroke. And I had no choice but to await my destiny.

...When there was only a month left till the date that the gypsy woman had set for my death, I discovered that my husband was having an affair. I wasn't surprised or angry, even:

71

I took it all in with great understanding, as if it were all happening to someone else.

I learned about the affair completely on accident, as it always happens. I had come to the library on one of my days off. The door to the office was open, and I heard voices. And I instantly figured out what they were talking about. It turned out that my Valera had been coming in to visit Nina Zalygina, who also worked at his research institute. I knew her well. I always liked Nina: she was beautiful, unmarried, sharp-tongued, but was always proper in her interactions with men, never overly affectionate. She was great at housework and tailoring, but never showed off her strengths. Instantly I weighed the outcomes in my head: they would be happy together—after my death. But I was mostly happy for my daughter—now I was no longer scared to leave her alone in the world.

It had already been half a year when Valera had started coming back home later—right when Yulenka had her first dreams at night. He'd sleep on the couch so as not to wake me. Sometimes he'd give an explanation in the morning: there's a big project deadline coming up, he had to burn the midnight oil; through all of this he came off completely genuine and happy as always.

Why hadn't he asked for a divorce? Of course, he was thinking of our daughter. But he probably took pity on me as well. I had been thinking about divorce as well—that would have been fairer to everyone. But soon I let go of that thought: I didn't want anything to change, didn't want to traumatize my daughter. And besides, I didn't have much time left.

...at the point, I had basically cut Valera out of my mind, barely spoke to him. And I turned all of my attention to my thirteen-year-old daughter. My husband had been going to work every day in the same little brown sweater. Then I felt a sudden pang of guilt and quickly washed and ironed all of his shirts, sewed on all the loose buttons. Valera didn't say anything, but understood me the way a man ought to understand his wife: came home from work early, bought a good bottle of wine for dinner. I pushed my own glass away, so he drank alone, pronouncing a simple little toast from our youth: "To you and to us!" He came to bed with me and was insistent and very gentle. I didn't push him away, all for the same reason—I didn't want to make any fuss, any sudden movements, didn't want to talk things out. But the next night, using not feeling well as an excuse and giving him a guilty smile, I took the couch myself.

My relationship with my husband became difficult to understand at first glance—before I had never imagined that something like this was even possible. He sensed that I was not well. And he knew that there was nothing he could do to help. Now he'd come home late only about twice a week. The other days he'd help out around the house, even cook. I didn't chastise him out loud—or even in my thoughts: it's clear that a strong, healthy man needs a woman. When he was home, more often than not I would simply lie on the couch, watching Valera and our daughter tenderly as if I were frozen in place. And I was quietly pleased: my husband never asked me for any explanations.

...Finally, in February (my favorite month of the year!) I turned thirty-five. I refused to have any guests over. Valera brought me a huge bouquet of roses. I made salads, aspic jelly, a beef roast (as you remember, there was never any meat in the stores, but my husband found ways of getting any groceries he wanted). I wanted to make this day memorable for him. It wasn't joyful—our house was never joyful. But it was calm and comfortable: we looked at the photos in our family albums, even danced around with our daughter. The whole evening—sorry to repeat myself—I wasn't thinking about myself: I could only think about my daughter, what her memories of these days would be.

I was still calm the next morning when I got up. I brought candies and a store-bought cake to the library. I listened to everyone's joking wishes, cracked some jokes myself, to everyone's great surprise. And again: for some reason I carried within me the feeling of a finally completed mission.

...It was in April when I last saw my parents in my dreams... It was Sunday, the print shop was closed. Our whole family (including me) was in our front yard. We were sitting at a big table covered by a faded checked table cloth. Mom had put on the samovar. We were drinking tea, eating grandmother's pastries—apple and cottage cheese. I was three—sitting up on the high chair, reaching everything on my own, slurping tea off my saucer like my grandmother. She was holding Bertochka, breaking off bits of pastry for her to nibble. Mother and father were singing a duet, deliberately not making eye contact for some reason. They were singing Jewish, Belarusian, and old Russian romances. Some of them I had never heard before, but strangely enough I could still recall every single word when I woke up. We sat at the table until dusk. Finally, everyone left except for me and my mom. Suddenly I turned into a grown-up in a blink of an eye, the same age as my mother. She approached me, tenderly patted me on the head, touched my cheek (I can still feel her hand, grown rough from doing laundry): "My poor girl!" Then she added: "Live, my dear daughter, live!"

...I never had these sorts of dreams again. After three weeks I stopped expecting them.

So, what happened to me after that? The typical story: I returned to the normal flow of life. And I changed, though I still think back on those years when I kept my secret inside me. I never told my husband any of this. Though now I think that he had figured it all out on his own... if not everything, then some very important part of it. For instance, the goal of all my anticipations. You know, sometimes Valera would answer a question that I had only asked him in my mind. Or finish my sentence based on a single word—always laughing.

As always, I never expected anything good from life, but somehow stumbled into a pretty lucky post-perestroika narrative: Yulenka graduated from the famous Bauman Moscow State Technical University, swiftly fell in love, got married to a Russian-American. We followed her to Boston. Valera got lucky here too—during his very first interview, his smile convinced his boss to hire him. With my Soviet library science education there wasn't much that I could do. I set up a Russian Sunday school—unwillingly, by some kind of inertia. And you know, it turned out to be a great business. Maybe because I actually got invested in my work. I invited bored former professors, directors, artists, painters—all feeling dejected and left by the wayside—to teach at my school. We don't just teach Russian language and literature, but also the history of Russian culture, Russian religions, art, manners, other languages, including dead ones. We got ourselves a great reputation—well-deserved, if I say so myself.

Sorry, I got carried away there. That's not what you're curious about, and that's not what still troubles me to this day. I never figured it out: did the fortuneteller make a mistake? It was probably my mistake. I know that everyone has a life line. Every religion, including Judaism, tells us that fate is predetermined, that we all have a mission in life, though we may not be fully aware of it until the very end, until our last breath. At the same time, we have free will... Nobody, no matter what happens, can draw any final conclusion from their life. You know, I recently heard a translation of a poem by Hirsh Glick, a poem that had become the anthem on Jewish guerilla fighters. Two lines really shocked me, burned themselves into my memory: "Never say that you are on your final path." Like the majority of Russian Jews, I don't know Yiddish, but I suddenly remembered, like an echo from my childhood: "glick" means "happiness." Tell me, what do you know about the author's fate?

I nodded and said that the poet, who had chosen this multivalent pseudonym for himself, was a prisoner in the Vilnius ghetto, then in a concentration camp in Estonia. He died trying to escape—in August of 1941, I think.

Traveler

In early 1992, Jerusalem was hit by a snow storm. The city hadn't seen a winter like that in about a hundred years. Pedestrians drowned in mounds of snow, cars turned pirouettes on the roads, the wind swiftly struck down all the palm trees. During that time, I was reading a manuscript that, much like the storm, brought me back to Russia. The byline was Ab Mishe, the title *Rough Draft*. The author was a recent expat from Moscow—the world knew him under the name Anatoly Abramovich Kardash.

This piece of writing unlike any other had its own strange fate. The manuscript was yet to be published as a standalone book, but many knew about it. At first, *Rough Draft* had become famous in samizdat. Then it started "making the rounds"—excerpted—in Russian and Israeli publications. Finally, the famous literary critic Lev Anninsky published a long and, as always, glowing article in a Moscow literary journal about "Ab Mishe's manuscript." The article really went for it: "...a colossal, thorough investigation of the Jewish question that touches all areas of humanistic inquiry and all stages of the thousand-year-long diaspora."

I must admit: it's difficult for me to introduce Ab Mishe's work to you, dear reader. It's difficult to capture the author's bold and audacious project. I'll begin by describing what was immediately obvious, what was surprising and concerning. Many chapters from *Rough Draft* consisted entirely of... quotes. At times quite lengthy, these excerpts took up several pages, flowing freely, interrupted only by brief (one to three sentences) comments by the author. Maybe this is an anthology? I asked myself. No, that's not quite right. The quoted texts were not neutral at all. Though they sometimes continued one another, they were more often in conflict with one another. Was the book an ongoing polemic with itself? But that wasn't quite right either. Moreover, the quotes weren't typically connected by some problematic, some idea, but by some association that didn't make itself apparent to the reader, by some image that had flashed through the author's memory.

But then one day, I suddenly figured it out: Ab Mishe had written a confession. Yes, a confession constructed in a manner we aren't used to whatsoever. The author often speaks using other people's words, but expresses something painfully his own.

Perhaps one would see a contradiction between the inner essence of this narrative and its literary form. However, there's no contradiction. We have before us a chronicle of an "investigation" into Jewish history. Or more accurately: a diary of cognizing the history of mankind through the prism of the Jewish people's fate. The subjective nature of the authorial perspective doesn't rule out a certain accuracy in delivering the material, but in fact only strengthens it. Of course, the "conclusions" of the investigation are known beforehand, but Ab Mise needs to verify them for himself. Such a task isn't for everyone: behind all of the scholarly formulas, the facts and figures, the political programs, the confusions of letters — there is blood. But Ab Mishe had taken up this task.

How and why did he come to the decision to begin his investigation? The answer, I think, is obvious. Anatoly Kardash, like all of us, belonged to the "silent" Soviet Jewry. We lived, forgetting our native language, not knowing our traditions, losing our national culture. But, as we know, the exodus from Egypt regularly recurs in Jewish history. This process always begins not with the feats of great leaders, but with an attempt at self-understanding and self-consciousness — understanding one's roots, one's close and distant past. With an attempt to defeat the slave within. Of course, such a process of self-knowledge is necessary for the people as a whole, if it wants to survive and find new breath.

And so, the attempt begins with a journey through a symbolic desert. Where was Ab Mishe's desert. The reader thinks back on Ancient Greece and Rome, Egypt, Spain, Portgula, France, Germany, Poland... But to be more precise, the first and main stop on this route is the Land of Antisemitism. Its contour is "the universal system of hatred," its borders "beyond geography and ethnography," easily stepping across "lands and souls." Without simplifying it at all, Ab Mishe sought to sketch an anatomical model of this system, exposing its foundations: ideology, history, legal systems. He examined its forms, mechanisms, fields of "operation" as well as the ways it manifested: science, public health, culture, love, leisure, school — of course, some of notions are colored by the author's own ironic stance. Ab Mishe also looked into specific historical figures: leaders, collaborationists, elites, ordinary citizens... Truly, an enormous country: in essence, Cain himself founded it, the offspring of "serpent seed." Jews have internalized the main rules for life within this country, made them part of their very genetic code: someone is always to blame for everything, someone foreign, defenseless — oftentimes a Jew. And so, travelling around different centuries, Ab Mishe kept finding the same thing: "...the blood of the slaughtered ran higher than the threshold of the synagogue." As a result: "a city is taken — pogrom. A village falls to invaders — pogrom. On route to the battle front — pogrom. On the path of retreat — pogrom."

It is notable that the "mystery" of antisemitism torments Jewish people first and foremost: the most self-hating flagellate themselves, attempting to find some sort of truth in what the people who hate them say, to understand the logic of their oppressors (this right here is the root of a Jew's own mysterious-seeming antisemitism). Pointless torments! Ab Mishe repeats over and again. Antisemitism, after all, is not the problem of the Jews themselves. It is a worldview, something of a litmus test for humanity as a whole. Antisemitism, according to Jean-Paul Sartre, whom Ab Mishe loves to quote,

is the "fear upon encountering the problem of human existence," the fear "of oneself, one's own consciousness, one's
own freedom, one's own instincts, one's own self-responsibil-
ity, loneliness, changes, society, and the world in general—in
a word, everything except Jews themselves." Moreover, "the
draw of antisemitism doesn't require any external stimula-
tion: it comes before any event that could provoke it, it in-
vents these events in order to find fuel for its fire..." History
can easily be used to confirm another of Sartre's theses: while
the image of the Jew is the most useful for the anti-Semite,
this phobia allows for substitutions of the object of hatred—
the role of Jews can be played by members of the intellectual
elite, Black people, Armenians, Roma... (nowadays the ruins
of the Soviet empire provide a diversity of options!)

Leading his search for truth in the labyrinths of the ev-
er-changing yet consistently cruel history of the Jewish people's treatment, Ab Mishe pondered the psychology of time
and the psychology of distinct personalities. The righteous
and the scoundrels, murderers and their victims, heroes and
bystanders. Ab Mishe is very sensitive to the way psychology
manifests itself in a turn of phrase, in a silence, in a slip of
the tongue. It is illuminating to follow the author through his
observations about the frivolous weaving of verbal lace when
government officials change their "perspective on the Jewish
question" with virtuosic ease. Or to observe how academics
and writers fall into the web of antisemitism. You can't talk
about Ab Mishe's masterful psychological prose without mentioning his chapter "Photograph." The entire chapter, running
eighty pages long, is not a genuine quote, but a masterful
imitation, behind which lies a dangerous truth. Immersing
himself in documentary material, Ab Mishe reconstructs
the thought processes and speech of a nameless participant
in the rebellion in the Warsaw ghetto. It's like we are looking deep into a photograph that afterwards travelled around
the world: a young woman in a man's cap, wearing a coat and
cheap beads. Next to her stands an SS officer, pointing his
machine gun at her. Somewhere close by is another: he wants

capture this scene—in order to remember it for a long time? She is just about to be murdered. But a few minutes before her death, she will tell future generations about herself and her comrades. "I am speaking in their voices now... I am not inventing a single fact, without adding anything, without any ornament for the sake of fame—I will not lie, I don't have the right, I just don't have the time to invent anything, I don't even have time to fix my cap. I only need to manage to tell it all while that guy is fiddling with his camera..."

There was another unique side to Ab Mishe's book. By itself it presented a rare and irreplaceable document for sociologists, psychologists, historians of Soviet Jewry. Scholars, for example, will be compelled to reread the list of authors that Ab Mishe "grilled" during his investigation: Leo Tolstoy, Lev Bezymensky, Lion Feuchtwanger, Vladimir Korolenko, Lydia Ginzburg, Zenon Kosidowski, Maxim Gorky, Ilya Ehrenburg, Anna Frank, Vassily Grossman, Martin Nilsen, Isaak Teneromo, Howard Melvin Fast, Eric Frank Russell... Names great and obscure, remembered and forgotten. Their books, articles, letters (at times only historical commentaries to other works) formed the consciousness of the Soviet Jew in the 60s-80s. They are characterized by the same turns of phrases, insights, and intellectual dead-ends as the author of *Rough Draft* himself.

Having completed the book, he embarked on perhaps the most important leg of his journey through the "desert." After finishing his project, he consciously wrote out his Jewish name—Ab Mishe—next to the title. What remained back there, in the "rough draft" of his life? His childhood: born in 1934 in Kyiv; after his father was sent to the camps, his mother was paranoid about getting arrested as well for a long time; he grew up in the provinces—first in Central Asia, in evacuation, then in villages and towns, where his then-released father was allowed to reside. His youth: I don't think he experienced much anti-Semitism; it was as if it didn't exist in Siberia—Anatoly studied at the automobile manufacturing institute in Omsk. Then suddenly in the middle of our conversation he recalled, like it was a dream: "For some reason, I was happy that

I didn't look like a Jew…" His adulthood: he worked in Kharkiv at a top-secret research institute, defended his dissertation; his life melted away, disappeared into oblivion, lost its meaning. In searching for this purpose, he was beset by questions: who am I in this world? Why have my people and I suffered so much? Is anti-Semitism eternal? How do you remain true to yourself in the dehumanizing state of totalitarianism?

This is where the pages of his diary begin. Here these "childish" questions become concrete, grow the flesh and bone of history. Throughout *Rough Draft* runs a melody— at times tender and lyrical, at times mocking and showy, at times mourning. I agree with Lev Anninsky: "this book is constructed based on excerpts from other texts—it is not "scholarly," it is musical from the first line to the last." I think this is an apt description of the spiritual precision that lies at the heart of *Rough Draft*: after all, music is the best tool to record a person's inner life, the movement of their soul.

…again, I return to the past. When he was twenty-eight, the doctors found a malignant tumor that had already started to metastasize. The situation was hopeless—one night Anatoly stole a look at the report and read his diagnosis. He told me about this, a little embarrassed, worried about getting too melodramatic: "…But I was absolutely sure that I would jump up, crawl out of this whole; when I got better, I tried to divine why fate had gifted me life."

After completing *Rough Draft*, Ab Mishe was able to answer this question. He had had an opportunity for self-reflection. Then he moved to Israel, took a job at the Holocaust memorial Yad Vashem. Years passed. He published his books, slowly attracting a readership— *Warning: Jews!*, *Rough Draft*, *Amid the War. Dedications*, *Right on the Black Sea*, and an anthology he compiled called *Holocaust. The Killing of Jews 1933–1945*.

But that's a different story. Remembering my first meeting with Ab Mishe in snowy Jerusalem, I often think: walking across the desert is easy when you remember the most important things: where you're coming from, and where you're going…

1992

And That's How It Was

It is difficult for me to read Samuil Esterovich's memoirs, even harder to make an attempt at understanding them... How can I explain this peculiarity of the reader's reception of this humble account of a Jew from Vilnius who survived the Shoah and many years later decided to describe "how it was"?

Truth is the simplest key to this mystery. Every line of Samuil Esterovich's text breathes its truth. The truth shocks the reader, often plunging them into a deep confusion. Indeed, I am drawn to those particularly "difficult" pages the most, my gaze lingering on them for a long time.

After narrating how he and his family hid in an underground bunker, the memoirist notes: "We truly had to pass through scenes straight out of Dante." The name of the great Florentine, who had strikingly exposed the depths of human existence, was not uttered in vain. Time and again Esterovich's memory tears out individual episodes from the past, where circumstances test man's core essence, where, at least from a birds-eye view, doubt is cast on eternal truths: humanism, morality, duty, love...

Here a woman betrays her loved ones to the Gestapo during an interrogation.

Here a Jewish man, in order to save himself, tells Hitler's police about his son from his Christian wife, a son who is serving in the German army.

During a "children's campaign," kids from the ghetto were led away to their death, and oftentimes parents just had to deal with it.

Hiding underground, people suffocate due to a lack of fresh air. Some lose their minds, their moans resounding through the hideouts, others murder their neighbors with bricks without a second thought: enemies are nearby, can't let them hear a sound...

Here I have listed only a couple Dante-esque scenes in Esterovich's lengthy manuscript. No, it's no coincidence that after the war many other former prisoners of the ghettos and concentration camps didn't like talking about what they had endured. Moreover, they hid the memories of the Shoah from themselves.

And still there's no escape from the age-old questions: should we be talking about this? will these constant reminders undercut the moral health of the nation, not the mention the nation in diaspora, whose national self-consciousness is already unstable?

"We have to tell the whole truth!" was Samuil Esterovich's answer to these questions, lying sick in bed in America, at the twilight of his life, looking back on the past. He knew with absolute certainty that truth never destroys, but strengthens a nation's character. Our descendants have a right to know about everything that befell us on our historical path. One cannot forcefully silence memory in order to protect a person's spiritual comfort... These are the commandments of the memoirist—simple and courageous. And the grateful reader from the future will be sure to accept them as well.

Another thing, for the sake of objectivity. It goes without saying that Samuil Esterovich's far-seeing memory also preserved many moments of heroism, loyalty, human dignity... The thing is that the author never really makes this explicit. Throughout his book, Esterovich has the tendency to make generalizations, "illuminate trends." And the most general trend that he sought out the most was the capital-t Truth. The reader is quick to pick up on this: the author does not resort to any broad stereotypes about any people as a historical actor, as is often the case. Like all Jews, Esterovich impatiently

awaited the arrival of the Red Army, but then became an impartial chronicler of the wave of antisemitism that engulfed
Russia at the end of the Great Patriotic War. The memoirist
mentions the good deals of individual Poles, to whom he owes
his life. But then other Poles come before his eyes—for example, auto workers that cheered at the sight of Jews being led to
their death. Esterovich is harsh critic of Lithuanians complic-
it in violence against Jews. Then he turns to a different story: during the German retreat the Esterovich family escaped
from the HKP labor camp (working class Jewish families were
held there, put to work on German auto repairs). A Lithuanian
man, a total stranger, approached them on the street—with
an offer to shelter them. He saved their lives! Finally, as the
reader is sure to realize, Esterovich does not idealize his own
people whatsoever.

At times it seemed to me that he was destined to survive
and live through so much in the years of the war first and
foremost so that he could tell his ancestors about it. He is able
to capture the reader's attention naturally, simply by narrating his fate. Esterovich is quite open and confessional in his
reminiscences. His daughter was able to give me further details about his life that added more brush strokes to his portrait. Samuil (Munya as those closest to him called him) was
born in Vilnius in 1897 to a "moderately well-off family" of
merchants. Educated in Petersburg and Germany, he became
a "successful businessman" himself by the start of World
War II. Under Soviet rule, as his daughter Perella told me,
Samuil was subject to persecutions as a "bourgeois"; when all
businesses and bank accounts were nationalized, he was unable to find himself a job that would have shielded him from
deportation. The majority of his apartment was taken over by
Communist bureaucrats. He was right on the edge of being
deported when Germany attacked Russia, its former ally.

That's when trials fell upon Samuil Esterovich one by one.
But it seemed as if fate itself was protecting him. The author
painfully returns to particular moral dilemmas, engendered
through his survivor's guilt, over the course of decades. At

one moment, his job as an autoworker saved him: the factory was giving out special permits, their own sort of "life-savers." But was it easy to feel truly alive? At the start of the German occupation in Ponary, two of Esterovich's sisters were shot in the massacre that ensued (they didn't have a "safe conduct"). Then his mother died as well. Thinking that Jews were only being killed in Lithuania, Esterovich manages to shuttle through his sisters Emma, Anna, and his niece Shella to Belarus. "The day they arrived," Perella writes, "they were herded into a synagogue and burned alive."

Who knows?—perhaps these constant spiritual torments and attempts to find some sort of reason in the tragic paradoxes of history, the drive to carry the cargo of facts, doubts, and thoughts into the future—perhaps all this at last awakened the chronicler's talent.

What happened to Samuil Esterovich after the war? For some time, he worked in Vilnius as an economist and, like his daughter notes, "went through tragicomical struggles with Soviet central planning." After that, "no longer wanting to live under Communist rule," the Esterovich family repatriated to Poland. Experiencing the full force of Polish anti-Semitism on himself, they fled for Italy. There, Perilla got her PhD in Chemistry, and Samuil worked at the Jewish Joint Distribution Committee as a refugee inspector, protecting people as helpless as he had just been, to escape "persecution and exploitation." The road, as they say, is the Jew's lot in life. After Italy—they emigrated to the States. The Esterovich family starts out in New York, Perilla gets married and moves to California, where her parents are finally persuaded to follow her after two decades of convincing.

...Again, I am trying to imagine Samuil Esterovich in this last part of his life. He is nonetheless pursued by loss: his wife had recently passed away. Finally, on his daughter's recommendation, he begins to write down his memoirs. Of course, it is difficult for him to overcome the nearly forgotten flow of the Russian language, to define a style. It was a lot easier for him to enter the past—it hadn't gone anywhere, remaining within him forever. What did he think about then? About the cruel century, about history that never seems to teach humanity much of anything? Of course, he remembered Vilnius, where he managed to return to shortly before his death.

Samuil Esterovich passed in 1985. Perella wrote and edited his memoirs, translated them into English, published them in the States with a small print run.

What more is there to add? Esterovich's notes came into my life about twenty years ago. Then a friend of mine Professor Irena Veisaitè[13] sent fragments of these memoirs into the Vilnius almanac *Jewish Museum*, which I was editing at the time.

Years passed. But I am still drawn to the "naïve" questions that Samuil Esterovich poses: how can we keep what is human within us? How do we live—and survive?

1994, 2006

A Single Letter

The life of the writer Iosif Rabin was long and happy... in my mind I repeat these cliched but seemingly quite appropriate words and feel them to be internally inconsistent. Almost blasphemous. Is it possible to say this about any Soviet Jewish writer?

Tragedy seemed to chase down these writers everywhere, all the time. Even if it seemed as if some of them got lucky. This is the way Iosif Rabin "got lucky." He died in 1988 in his own bed, not in a jail cell or camp (he landed there at the end of the "legendary" year of 1937 as a "Polish spy"). He survived the battlefront, where he fought as a member of the Rifle Regiment. He managed to publish many books that brought him fame. He was beloved by his family, friends, readers ("Oh, Rabin's Yiddish is just magical!" as my acquaintance, now an old woman, recently sighed)... And still here I will cut short this list of false moments of well-being! The very tragedy I speak of lived in every one of these moments — daily and imperceptible.

I often thought about that, when in the late 80s/early 90s I started to write down the memories of Jewish writers, their widows and children. That's how I met Iosif Rabin's daughter — Liubov Iosifovna Zak.

My frequent meetings with Liubov in Moscow and Lithuania took place with society rapidly changing in the background: as always, these changes did not bode well for Jews. Swift pogroms seemed to be the norm as was the total collapse of the economy (for which, of course, the Jews were blamed). In such times, who needed those books printed with the ancient letters of the Hebrew alphabet? How could these Jewish manuscripts be saved from the flame of utter chaos? There was no good answer. Still, I advised Liubov to place her father's archive in the hands of the Jewish Museum, recently resurrected in a newly independent Lithuania: "They are experts in preservation." There was another reason as well — Iosif Rabin wrote a lot about Vilnius, the city that has long been called the "Jerusalem of Lithuania," the city that he loved — not hiding his tenderness.

On a number of occasions, I saw Liubov packing the archival folders for the road. She was bidding farewell, leafing through the pages of her father's and, in part, her own life.

...A while ago, I had been working with author's archives for many long years. It seemed that Iosif Rabin's archive was different from those I had encountered before. Reading through the manuscripts of published works, you could observe the author moving from concept to execution. Rough drafts and outlines are the deepest secrets of the verbal artist, along with letters from colleagues, old friends, and readers... No, no, this was a special archive — the archive of a Jewish writer.

How many materials didn't make it in! Either confiscated by KGB officers during a search or destroyed by the writer himself, as he was anticipating the possibility of the next arrest. As I was reading, I was struck by the feeling that the majority of these materials were "reserved" right from the onset — conceived for a particular kind of silence. Even the letters. Their addressees were long deceived (as were most of the correspondents, most likely). But why then — decades later even — could I feel the aura of anxiety and fear that emanated from them? There was no doubt that these letters' every word was intended to be read by the KGB as well. Soviet Jews had mastered the art of subtle communication, relying on mere hints and suggestions. Formally speaking, there was nothing suspicious about the message — only the "true" addressee could correctly understand the second, hidden meaning of each sentence... Some of Iosif Rabin's correspondents had a characteristic "forgetfulness." Their envelopes often lacked a return address or a sender's surname. Many wrote like that, telling themselves that this precaution wouldn't hurt anyone and that it was in everyone's best interest to avoid having their name read by a KGB agent one more time...

The archive of the "Soviet Jewish writer" provokes thinking about the psychology of his creative process and, no less importantly, about the psychology of his existence and survival. This topic deserves to become the subject of a lengthy scholarly study... In fact, I realized one day, a single letter from Iosif Rabin's archive can eloquently and clearly give an exploration of this very tragedy.

Alas, not all letters were so friendly: among the messages received by Jewish writers in the Soviet Union some were explicitly antisemitic. Even during those relatively calm years when "collective protests" against "rootless cosmopolitanism," "white-coat murders," and "Zionist conspirators" died down, many readers were irked by the mere presence of a Jewish author's name on the front cover of a book, by a character's markedly Jewish name, by these literary characters seeming to be... just like "normal" Russians.

I waivered for a long time before finally deciding to publish one of these letters in the "Jewish Museum" almanac (Vlinius, 1994): did I dare risk multiplying the potential for antisemitic nonsense with the help of the printing press? But then I remember how Iosif Rabin himself read and read this very letter: an author always feels pressure surrounded by hostility and suspicion — ideas grow dim, inspiration evaporates... I didn't change the style or any of the spelling choices of the letter. The date on the envelope read August 28, 1957.

The letter was anonymous. The author, like a few other of Iosif Rabin's (Jewish) correspondents, disappeared into the shadows... but for a completely different reason. From context it was clear that the author was an older woman. She had read Rabin's collection *Novellas and short stories* published a year ago in Russian. And "couldn't help but take up the pen":

I am moved to write this letter by great indignation and anger.

I read your stories and novellas completely by accident—"At Neman," "Philip the Weasel," "The Tractor-Driver," "Profession," "Nema Liubich," "Home," "Source," "Girlfriends," "Housewarming," and "New Year"—and was shaken to my very core.

There's a limit to everything. Everyone knows very well the role that Jews played during the Great Patriotic War. They were never on the front lines, and even if they were, those are random cases—one Jew for every hundred thousand Russians. Why not write the truth about Jews, about their cowardice, lowliness, thievery, and dirty ways? Anyone who reads your book will be indignant. The audacity!!! Where? When? It's better not to write a single word than to subject us to this outright heresy. And Jews wonder why people don't like them. Everything that is low and disgraceful is contained in that race. If there are any good ones out there—they're one in ten thousand. You can't be impartial reading this book. It'd be a disservice, more harm than good. All the facts point to the opposite. It goes against everything. Only some provocateur could've written a book like this, to get everyone riled up against the Jews even more. It'd be better if Rabin went back to his yid grocery store, back to his yid stand at the market, rather than to continue to elevating these dirty fucking kikes. All yid women stink like goats. And the Russian people will never be rid of these vermin. I don't support Hitler, but too few Jews have been wasted, we need to beat them till they're no more.

It was impossible to respond to a letter like that. And not just because there was no return address. It was impossible to respond to it in the public sphere too. Iosif Rabin knew that every censor and editor would interpret any serious discussion of the "Jewish question," issues around Jewish national identity and consciousness as a result of militant anti-Semitism the same way: as a transgression, as "Zionist propaganda," "bourgeois nationalism."

And so, the author remained silent, sensing the thickening of the gloomily approaching wave of state anti-Semitism. A writer trying to understand everyone could have stopped to think: what experiences led this woman to such a violent out-burst? What brought her to the conclusion that Jews were the cause of all her problems? And who was actually benefiting from these sentiments continue to survive in society?

According to his daughter, Iosif Rabin had no doubts that the opinion of this anonymous letter-writer could not be equated with "everyone's" opinion like she wanted it to be. He did, however, have to consider all possible reactions to his books, including these ones. He was clearly conscious of the fact that anti-Semitism was a fact of life for the "life and work" of a Jewish writer in this country.

I was also struck by the strangely phantasmagorical na-ture of the situation. In his deeds, not only in his words, Rabin was a "staunch internationalist." In his youth he led the un-derground Vilnius city council of the Komsomol, at one point he was considered a proletarian writer, many of his books "reflected the history of the Jewish worker's movement prior to the October Revolution" and praised the Revolution in ro-mantic overtones (cf. the encyclopedia). And then he had col-lided with cynical reality: "yid," "kike."

Of course, Rabin was aware that, aside from tortuous si-lence, there was another way out of the situation—some pro-tested in public, others left for Israel... But this is where I will end my essay. Looking in from a different epoch, we are not the ones to answer yesterday's painful questions. Moreover, a heavy silence about the most sacred was perhaps the truest, always remaining tragedy of the Soviet Jewish writer.

All I can add as a conclusion: Rabin kept this very letter for thirty years. As a reminder to himself?

Not Remembering It All...

To the memory of Dina Kharik —
With great thanks for the lessons in optimism

I didn't understand this right away: she doesn't like talking about the camps, prison, about her own arrest and, of course, about her husband's arrest.

She doesn't protest, she lets me ask my questions without interrupting. Every time, without fail, imperceptibly—perhaps even to herself—she changes the topic of conversation.

She looks young and elegant. She looks like those people who keep themselves from aging with all their will. I don't even think about figuring out how old she is. Or rather, I don't get the opportunity to do so: she smiles, and her smiles await my answer.

It seems she had become accustomed to talking only about happy things—or pleasant things, at the very least—a long time ago. She had become accustomed to finding the same grand reason in any situation: everything is for the best!

The first time I discovered this habit of hers, I was climbing the steep staircase that led to her apartment. Suddenly I heard:

"We don't have an elevator—it's so great!"

She added, noticing my surprise:

"It's terrific exercise—even a few times a day!"

Her apartment doesn't have a balcony? Another bonus: you won't get used to lounging on a chaise-lounge, blankly staring out onto the street... No, she can't live like that! She goes to the park every day—not just for fun, of course: "You know, there are these old ladies that don't keep up with the news. I, on the other hand, read the most interesting stuff in the freshest newspapers!"

Among the stories she loves to tell, the one about how she met her future husband, a famous Jewish poet, is particularly notable.

It's a story full of melodrama, but without any hint of the future tragedy to come:

"Okay... so... I had just graduated from the Jewish pedagogic institute. I got a job in Minsk, in Jewish kindergarten No. 3. I was living with a friend of mine, on Ostrovsky Street. Then one day in August... yes, in August... I'm on my way to work. Suddenly I see a man walk from the neighboring apartment complex: black curly hair, an elegant pince-nez... A thought flashes like lightning through my mind: "Now that's a poet!" I stop to take a look at him. I can feel his gaze on me, so I get embarrassed and keep walking. But, to my surprise, I hear his footsteps behind me..."

I'm interested in her story, though I have heard this story — at least its general outline — many times before and had even read in a Minsk literary journal. Still, I'm curious to figure out why this plot is so significant to her.

"...He's being all cute and flirty: "Where'd I meet you earlier? You seem so familiar." I'm silent, more flustered than I've ever been before. Then he poses the same question a different way: "Don't you think you've seen me before somewhere?" Now I suddenly get a surge of bravery! And I start laughing: "I don't think so. I've seen you on the book jacket photos of your books, at a poetry reading at the Jewish pedagogic institute..." "Yes, yes," he nods, "at the reading. That's where I noticed you too." *Oh yes,* I think to myself, *Guess sitting in the second row really paid off!*"

Here she pauses, preparing me for an unexpected turn:

"You know though, this turned out to be a lie! When we got married, my husband confessed that he made it all up... right on the spot!"

Her laugh is ringing, doesn't sound like an old lady's laugh at all. Her name rings out too: Dina.

No, she doesn't forget where she left off in telling her story. And she confident goes on. I compare her memory and my own. No big discrepancies. It seems like all the details of her story are carefully calculated and weighed out. Weighed out on the scales of an optimism rarely found nowadays. That's why the details don't really change themselves. Only their order changes—like individual words and sentences.

In everything else (everything that doesn't disrupt the major key), she is light and free. For example, she doesn't avoid the facts that she thinks could be uncomfortable: "We can forgive a poet some of his transgressions, no?"

It turns out the poet was a lot older than her! Almost twice her age. And he was very worried—would she agree to be with him? ("You know he had a lot of groupies. After we got married, I saw that he had a whole suitcase full of fan mail. Among these letters, many from women who were in love with him. One of these groupies served time in the same camp as me. But I guess I was a special case: this love had shaken him to his core!") At times he waivered: would the marriage be stable? Perhaps that's why he arranged a traditional wedding ceremony, with a matchmaker and everything. He invited his friend, the poet Zelik A. and his own father to come and "evaluate" his bride.

"...And, you know what, he was up to his old tricks again! He was so sneaky about it! He pretended as if Zelik and his father were just stopping by right when I was at his place. "Well, well, well, what a coincidence!" And just as "coincidentally" he had the best snacks right at that time!"

She quips. She laughs. Her eyes shine with youth.

In her published memoires, I am struck by the strange proportions of the text sizes: how Dina met herfuture husband, their first dates, their marriage takes up two thirds of the whole book. She doesn't mention her own tragedy at all. And censorship has nothing to do with it! The memoires were published in 1988—you were allowed to talk about Stalinist repressions at that time. It was even "fashionable" to shout about them at the top of your lungs. But she remained silent.

Anyways, I noticed that even her own children received but a passing comment. (She dedicated the second largest section to a trip to Moscow with her husband in 1937 for the Pushkin Jubilee).

"What happened to your children?"

Maybe, she wants to cringe at my tactlessness, but she resists. And she doesn't avoid my question — she tells me about them precisely, but without great emotion.

When she got arrested in November 1937, the boys stayed behind with a young worker named Manya. Then they got sent off somewhere — probably to a special orphanage for the children of "enemies of the people." Their last names were changed, as was custom, so the boys wouldn't have been able to find her, even if they survived. Yulik was three, Dodik was a year and eight months...

When she was released in 1956, she went looking for them herself — she searched long and was ultimately unsuccessful.

"Yes, there are records," said the homeland security office, "But we don't know where they are. They probably died."

"Died," she repeats.

Of course, I nod, they died. How can she keep on living, keep on surviving if she thinks otherwise?

Legends circulated about the fate of the poet. Some of them were forgotten. Everything was quite simple — the people who cared all died.

All versions agreed on one point: the poet lost his mind in prison.

Maybe he was tormented by that utter lack of logic?

In his verses, he had sung the praises of the October Revolution, of the Red Army where he had served. He was sincere: when he joined the Party, he had dedicated all his energy to the building of a new culture, served as a member of the Belarusian Academy of Science and the Executive Committee of the Union of Soviet Writers, member of the Executive

Committee of and chairmen of the Jewish section of Union of Belarusian Soviet Writers... A prestigious list, though incomplete.

They say that the poet banged against the walls of his cells for days on end, shouting the same phrase in Yiddish and Russian: "*Farvos? Za chto?* What for?"

Naturally, there was no answer.

She confirms: yes, that's how it happened. Then she continues, speaking quickly and looking off at the window.

The poet began growing increasingly bewildered with his position long before his imprisonment, of course. He couldn't understand why he was getting harassed at meetings, why his friends were getting arrested.

It was his turn in 1937. He was staying at the Pukhovichi Writer's House[14] at the time. Late one evening, they showed up to his apartment in the city. They dug through all his belongings, sealed up all the rooms, leaving Dina and the kids to stay in the office.

A month later, completely unexpectedly, she received a letter from her husband: *I am not guilty; hope that they'll sort everything out; I'll see you soon, take care of the kids.*

Many years later, the poet's cellmate told her that the price he paid for that letter was a confession to all sorts of fake "crimes."

The package she attempted to get to him was not let through. The poet was shot in Minsk on October 29, 1937. "What do you think?" she asks me, "Maybe they didn't want to keep housing a madman at the prison?"

They told her that before the execution they took him to the bathhouse with the other prisoners. There, unaware of what he was doing, he burned himself with the hot water, moaning, yelling—suffering. "Maybe they just didn't want to treat him, didn't want to deal with him?"

The old grief hits her like an ocean wave. But she manages to regain her balance, quite skillfully.

"...I was also in prison," she tells me, offering me a hand pie, "...Tasty, right? They're really delicious if you have them with some juice."

She offers me pomegranate juice, pouring some boiling water over my cup before handing it to me. A teakettle is permanently whistling on her stove. This is a habit, after she caught brucellosis in the camps. "It's really good for you! You can always guarantee that all the bacteria are killed off."

She didn't go through many rounds of questioning. Her situation was clear to the authorities: she was the wife of an enemy of the people[15].

She once asked the investigator, "How'd this happen? The poet was writing perfectly Soviet poems." The investigator was condescending: "The poems were Soviet, but the author was not."

When she returned to Minsk nineteen years later, it turned out that most of her relatives had perished in the war as they were being evacuated (only her sister was saved by some miracle).

But her husband's friends, especially Petrus Brovka[16], helped her out a lot. She got an apartment, republished the poet's collections... "With the royalties, I got myself this." She gestures at her small room, which at first seems to be very lavishly decorated, but, in reality, is very modest. She's especially proud of her old piano:

"Imagine that, I still play to this today! I did forget a ton in the camps—both my Yiddish and my solfege. But it was a fun challenge—to reacquire and restore what had been lost. But I never got my English back."

When in the early 90s I travel from Vilnius to Minsk from time to time, Dina Zvulovna is sure to invite me to come over.

She really understands the importance of my undertaking: writing down the stories of the Jewish artists, of their spouses and children...

Could we meet at the Jewish library, which she runs?

"No, no, you should come over to my place... This city is unfamiliar to you, I'll warm you up with some tea. Just yesterday I bought some really tasty candy!"

At tea, she reads me some more of the poet's verses, this time in translation by Anna Akhmatova:

> I do not grieve, unloved by earthly fame,
> No one is kissing every step I take...
> Now, as all hearts become engulfed in flames,
> My verses form a mouth drawn taught by rage.

I am not surprised to find the poet to offer a prophecy: the poem was written in 1925, but it seems that he foresaw his own fate.

I am captivated by incongruousness of the tone of the stanza and the optimistic intonation of his wife's young, feminine voice.

The teakettle goes on whistling on the stove.

...Years later, I will realize that the image of this poet that carries the heavy weight of the truth is an integral part of the story of his ageless wife.

This image will "catch up with me" in Chicago—that's where I will meet and befriend the art historian and translator Vankarem Nikiforovich;[17] once he will read me his own translation of the poet's work "Evening":

> Evening... The dew is warm.
> The gloom has hidden everything.
> I softly wander down the earth
> Only my shadow following.
>
> My step is careful as I tread —
> The grasses sleeping in the meadow.
> I must stay silent, I understand,
> But can't help singing as I go.
>
> I should not live with these regrets
> And should just wait until the dawn.

But this desire grips my every thought…
Lord, just let me finish my song.

But let me return to the summer of 1991, to Minsk.

I am travelling for business to the Museum of the Great Patriotic War. Dina Zvulovna offers to show me around and help me out—introduce me to the museum workers, among whom she has a couple friends.

A sunny day. We walk on the main street for a long time—more than an hour. And that's when she takes pity on me, offering to teach me how to make yourself light and cheerful at will. She wants to gift me this feeling forever. She tells me about her morning calisthenics routine (the routine is simple enough; she thinks she's discovered some "genius" techniques that have existed for a long time). "…After you've done your "water regimen" you have to towel yourself a special way—not head to toe, but toe to head!"

I don't ruin her mood even when I mention her time in the camps. Of course, talking about that on a day like this won't do at all. It is impossible to talk about the camps cheerfully. But even here she manages to find an optimistic angle. All sorts of wonders happened to her in the camps! For example, she was miraculously healed of her brucellosis after being unable to stand for a year. God had always protected her in the camps, saving her right at the last possible moment. On a number of occasions, she was spared from horrible violence and rape.

"…Once I was "on duty" for my barrack. Everyone was supposed to leave for work. I was the only one who stayed behind along with the Kazakh overseer. I knew he was a rapist. What could I do? A good friend of mine (older than me) ran over to the medical center to ask the doctor, an older Jew, to sit with me… That's when he told me that the overseer had stage 3 syphilis, that many of the women he infected were being sent off to different camps…"

She remembered other instances of being miraculously saved. But then she came to and smiled, as if erasing her own story from her mind: "...You know, everything bad that happens in this life is like a dream. Don't you think?"

Leaning on my arm, she walks energetically, almost skipping in time with my words.

Is what happens next some sort of symbol?

Right as we are about to enter the museum, she suddenly flies forward, her hand losing its grip on my elbow.

And now she's stretched out on the pavement, a huge bruise on her cheek, her leg badly beat up. I help her up before running into the museum to get iodine and a bandage to dress her wound.

She refuses to get a cab. On the trolleybus she continues telling me something like nothing had happened... No complaints, just her typical laughter.

I am struck by the realization that this is the general schema for her life: a fall, a wound, a smile.

1992, 2003
(So that the reader doesn't have to go digging through
encyclopedias, I'll let you know:
my companion is Dina Zvulvna Kharik, the widow of the
poet Iza Kharik[18])

The Flight of a Lone Bird

In the first days of March 1998, I received a thick stack of typewritten sheets from Germany. They comprised the memoires of Vladimir Ilyich Porudominsky. By a strange, even symbolic, coincidence, the account was titled "In early March." Perhaps the subtitle will make things clearer — "Family trifles in 1953" — the year Stalin died.

In Chicago spring is the only time of year when I can breathe calm and easy. But reading with Porudominsky's notes was suffocating: the text was imbued with an unavoidable and bitter air of fear, like smoke from a crematorium. Vladimir Porudominsky recounted his tortured path to finding a job at the height of the "doctor's plot." The young Jewish man, upon returning from the army after having studied editing in college, felt a dense yet invisible wall that now stood between him and the rest of the world. But what were the words "family trifles" doing in the title? "Of course, these are all trifles," the author seemed to insist, "...my conscience doesn't permit me to call them anything else in the time and space, where, glancing around myself, I can't help but see human suffering, grief and ruin."

I started thinking about this memoirist's rare talent: his unbelievably elastic style grasped and united so many striking figures, random phrases, and deliberate silences into a single group portrait of an epoch, when so much had to be read between the lines of a party newspaper. All these memories laid the foundation for Porudominsky's truly unique and wonderous prose.

It is often debated what a writer gains from the experience of emigration. Typically, most opinions are pessimistic. But I often recall the old Porudominsky, who became especially daring in his writerly experiments having emigrated.

Filling out a questionnaire, Porudominsky reflected: "To be honest, when I left Russia, I was certain that my professional life was over and foresaw a completely different plan for the rest of my time on earth. But, on the contrary, here I feel free, emancipated from all that oppressed me and prevented me from expressing myself fully 'back home'."

Some might be surprised by this confession—it might appear as if the author is rejecting his old works. I will say that Porudominsky's Soviet publication didn't have a hint of "selling out." He wrote for the popular book series "The Lives of Distinguished People," "Lives in Art," "Writers on Writers," helping thousands, if not millions, of readers discover the biographies, destinies, and artistic worlds of Vladimir Dal and Vsevolod Garshin, of Nikolai Ge and Mikhail Vrubel, of Karl Bryullov and Nikolai Yaroshenko, of Ivan Kramsky and Aleksandr Polezhaev, of Ivan Puschin and Aleksandr Afanasiev, of Nikolai Pirogov and Ivan Golikov...

And yet Vladimir Porudominsky was absolutely right to speak of his newfound "freedom" in emigration.

Speaking about his work, I often recall the way members of the Serapion Brothers, the 1920s Petrograd literary circle, greeted one another: "Hello, brother! Writing is so difficult..." It's helpful to reflect, however—what's so difficult about it? Naturally, it's not just the process itself, the dragging of the proverbial quill across the page or sitting at the computer for hours, trying to find the right image. It's a lot harder to find— within yourself!—new creative opportunities, harder to depart from a past self. A lot harder to "begin anew" with every work, as if your decade-long career never happened.

I often wondered why the kind of prose Porudominsky started writing in emigration has yet to be truly appreciated, why his writerly discovered have yet to be examined critically. I see two reasons. First, almost everything published by émigré writers typically gets ignored by reviewers in the home country—they see us as writing from some boring, far-off backwater. Second, Porudominsky's writing have a certain quality to them that make them particularly unobtrusive.

In an introduction to Podurominsky's "Waking up in the Night," Tatiana Bek, a wonderful poet and critic herself, described her attempts to find the key to the "mystery" of his prose, whose genre she struggled to define: "Fiction of high verisimilitude? Autobiographical essays? A verbal portrait en plen air? In any case—before us stands a prime example of lyrical prose, whose protagonist-narrator is very close to its biographical author. However, an exact equivalence cannot be drawn because the narrator is not egocentric. He condenses time, space, and history within himself..."

I'm not sure if Porudominsky ever truly formulated the main topic of his experiments. But it's clear that he was especially committed to an artistic *investigation of memory*. One of his characters, whose voice can easily be identified with Vladimir Ilyich's own, thinks to himself "Sometimes I think we don't recall the past because we want to, but because it forcefully reminds us. After all, it's only alive as long as we are alive... The fewer of us left, the narrower it gets—it leaves, stops existing along with us." This is one of the many definitions of memory that Vladimir Porudominsky gives throughout his works. This definition is the basis of so many plots for his novels and stories—"Grandmother's Funeral in the Winter of 1953," "Waking up in the Night," "A Pitstop on the Way to Paris," "Recently," "A Feast for Shades," "Private Lessons."

These pieces captivate me by how they capture the *flow* of life. At times this flow is turbulent and unpredictable. But looking back you begin to notice a definite life *plan*, albeit one that doesn't jump out at you immediately. I felt this when I read one of Podurominsky's first stories "The Unfinished Sonata." The heroine, a pianist, vainly attempts the question: why, for what purpose did she survive the Holocaust? She tries to find some higher meaning in what happened to her—in the ghetto, the young wunderkind was saved by her musical talent. And the meaning of it all appears to be simple—searching for the answer to this overwhelming question and expressing her search through music. "After twenty years of wandering, she realized, first with her senses, then with her mind, that only travelling the whole wide world is she truly at home..." Slowing down, the heroine "begins to feel like a bee she once saw at the entomological reserve: this bee lived in the hive, but was separated from its cluster by a glass wall." The heroine took on the strange inevitability of life's *rhythm*. Yet she didn't realize that this rhythm was the *answer* to her question.

The Holocaust highlights and intensifies the theme of memory.

The flow of life that suddenly reveals a higher truth takes our breath away in the Porudominsky's minor masterpiece "Rosenblatt and Zinger." The piece's origins as a memoir places the reader in close proximity to the narrative. Here they are before us—two donkey drivers in Tashkent. In a twist of fate, the former wealthy linen salesmen in Berlin and Vienna now don't even have a bed—they sleep on the floor under a winding staircase, lying atop "some mess of hay and rags." However, having escaped the Nazis, they arrived at some higher truth and are trying to convey to a Jewish teenager from Moscow. Thankfully, this young man speaks German. He is despondent: after being evacuated, he encountered anti-Semitism for the first time, though he had often heard "from his relatives that in the Soviet Union, everyone had forgotten that they were Jews..." The higher truth the two men have found is thousands of years old, though people are determinately pushing it away from themselves. "...Rosenblatt looked at me apologetically; his eyelids were bright red from the sun. 'My boy,' he repeated, 'forgetting is a mutual thing. We ourselves once forgot we were Jews. I would don a black tuxedo and a top hat, get a cab to church. The Germans would smile at and say 'Guten Tag.' But the day after Hitler came to power, it turned out that Germans never forgot that I was a Jew. They didn't say 'Guten

Tag' to me anymore. My boy, you can't forget that you're Jewish before others do.'"

Why did Jewish identity suddenly take center stage in Porudominsky's work? The author gives his answer in one of his articles: "Martin Buber writes that the Jews were 'a community based on memory'."

...At sleepless hours, I often remind myself these days: it's already morning in Cologne. I'd ask myself: what's my oldest friend doing now? Any news? Of course, I thought about the "mystery of Porudominsky." This mystery, of course, doesn't lie in the difficult coordinate system of his prose, but in the brilliant and ever enigmatic victory of his creative spirit over time itself that cruelly throws away our works and days like calendar pages.

Once Porudominsky co-authored a piece on Pushkin's Boldino autumn with the historian and writer Natan Eidelman. There's no doubt that emigration became his personal Boldino. I won't even try to list everything he wrote in those years.

For eight years Vladimir Porudominsky edited a truly unique diary, kept by his uncle Grigory Shur in the Vilnius ghetto. After it got published, the final version was translated into multiple languages and was a great success. Vladimir Ilyich later wrote: "My intimate familiarity with the documents from the Shoah is one of the most important experiences of my life." I will add that the piece is a prime example of quiet, but frequently thrilling Jewish prose.

I was not at all surprise to learn that, in addition to the universal pain of the Jews, Porudominsky was also drawn to German pain back then. Vladimir Ilyich began working on the book *Planck, son of Planck: Fragments of an Unwritten Diary* as if inspired by hearing someone's quiet voice. As it turned out, the life records of Erwin Planck were stored in the house where Vladimir's family had settled. Erwin's life story was tragic: the son of famous physicist Max Planck, he was a brilliant politician of the Weimar Republic. After Hitler's rise to power, he participated in the German Resistance before being executed in 1944 for the attempted assassination of the Fuhrer.

It was emigration that Porudominsky finally completed his yearslong work on Tolstoy. I've got all three of Vladimir Ilyich's books, dedicated to the great author. I remember that I was particularly taken with Porudominsky's *The Hues of Tolstoy*—a fascinating study how the colors the author uses indicate changes in his characters' moods. His book *If I Live or Leo Tolstoy on the Medical Sciences* is a favorite of mine. I return to it time and again, revisiting Tolstoy's universe with its dialectics of body and soul.

The reader generally doesn't recognize the author in his characters and plots. Porudominksy titled one of his best books *The Lone Bird on a Housetop*, taking a cue from the Psalms. I read this as a quiet confession, as the artist's formulation of his "life and works."

...All of us, writers included, come into this world with a special mission that we must discover and fulfil. This thought resounds in Porudominsky's books about various contributors to Russian culture. But he always avoided speaking about his own "special mission," eschewing any kind of pathos.

I called him a few days after the passing of Nadezhda Vasilievna—his wife and friend, a person endlessly dear to him. Even an ocean away I still felt how hard it must be for him now. But Vladimir Ilyich was pensive, clearly thinking about something: "Nadya is free, she has completed her assignment."

Only a person who devoutly believes in the Creator and His higher designs could have uttered those words.

A Man and His Fate
"On the Other Side of Words"

In the mid-80s, when I met the Lithuanian poet Alfonsas Bukontas, I didn't anticipate that this meeting would force me to reconsider much of my life up to that point...

Perhaps my reflection might appear strange, even to Bukontas himself. What did this mean: to truly change the course of another person's life? Bukontas even avoided making sudden movements and winced at the sound of loud voices. He had continued his existence for many decades quietly, preferring "to keep to the shadows." Lithuanian readers knew Bukontas as a unique lyric voice and as a brilliant translator of ancient and modern poetry. Curiously, however, he never engaged in the discourse, shied away from public debates, spent months without setting foot in the Writer's Union, at times would disappear from view altogether. His friends would even start betting—did Alfonsas return to his native village, was he just not picking up the phone...

It seems that I have drawn the portrait of a typical shut-in. But it's not that simple. From his teenage years, Bukontas learned to toss aside the cares of the world because he got used to the daily anticipation of death. And death could arrive at any minute.

His heart disease in many ways defined his personality, his way of life, but, at the same time, sharpened his perception of the world... His personality did stay the same even after the miracle: the German journalist Mariana Butenschon wrote a series of articles about Alfonsas, raised money for him to come to Germany, found a surgeon who'd perform the operation for free... Recently, Bukontas wrote to me: "It's been ten years since the operation, each of these years has been a gift."

But I'm getting ahead of myself. I remember, back in the 80s, the wonderful Ukrainian poetess Sofia Maidanskaya, with whom I frequently discussion the joining of the cosmic and national in creative expression, kept telling me:

"You absolutely have to meet Alfonsas Bukontas..."

I didn't really understand why she was so insistent. Perhaps, like many poets, she possessed the gift of foresight.

Those years I was immersing myself in Judaism, began writing down the oral narratives of Soviet Jews. Multiple generations (millions of people), I thought, will sink into oblivion never having told the bitter truth about themselves and the time, when the very word "Jew" was in essence unutterable in the national languages of the USSR... It seemed the history of "the Jews of Silence" (as the Nobel Laureate Elie Wiesel called his brethren in the Soviet Union) is full of mysteries.

Now would be the time to mention: the life of Alfonsas Bukontas began with a mystery. A mystery that remained unsolved for many years.

1

In Judaism we have the concept of "rescued children." The term automatically resounds with a sharp pain in my mind. The fact that the term is a metaphor—describing people raised away from their national traditions—doesn't make it any less painful. Alas, most Jews, born in the Soviet Union lived as "rescued children"...

The case of Bukontas is quite typical and truly unique at the same time. Alfonsas told me his life story a number of times, and once I managed to record it on tape. His tale could easily fill up a grand novel, but I will try to recount it briefly.

For a long time, his documents stated he was born on September 11, 1941 in the village of Dapšiai in the Mažeikiai District Municipality of the Lithuanian Soviet Republic to the family of Jeronimas and Marija Bukontas. Right away I will note that these people were saints—they really saved the child's life. Nevertheless, this information was completely false. Alfonsas learned the truth bit by bit only as a teenager: his real parents were Jewish. In 1954 he moved to the neighboring town of Židikai to continue his studies. He discovered that many of the town's denizens remembered his father the lawyer, his mother the dentist, his six-year-old brother, all of whom perished during the war. Alfonsas had already fallen in love with literature. It turned that the town library he frequented was where his family had lived before the war...

I am shocked by this story, not only by its tragic plot, but also by how natural and normal it seemed to everyone involved. How natural it was for Vaclovas Martinkus, the local Catholic priest, to develop and implement a plan for the Jewish child's rescue: sending him to a faraway village, baptizing him there, all the while holding his own in the face of police interrogation. Lithuanian fascists threatened to execute the families of Marija Bukontas and Elena Lauraitienė, but they did not waiver, refusing to give up the child. Jeronimas Bukontas was embroiled in a difficult and deadly game: trying to bribe German soldiers and policemen with money, vodka, and endless feasts... But ultimately, this strategy was his demise: when Lithuania was liberated by the Red Army, Jeronimas was arrested, accused of "collaborating with the Germans." He never returned from the camps.

We can't forget that there's another important plotline here: the story of the Jewish boy's soul, so to speak. This plotline mostly developed after the war.

The Jewish thinker Rebbe Rashab once said that each person consists of three layers—the "inner person," the "middle person," and the "outer person." No matter what we experience, no matter how life may break us down, only the two outer layers can be damaged. The "inner person" will forever remain untouched. In the story I recorded on my tape recorder, Alfonsas reconstructs the life of his "inner person" with surprising accuracy. Here are a couple excerpts from my recording:

The real world of my childhood was our big house in the village. It was almost a living creature to me. I knew well its every sound, remembered its every smell. It seemed enormous to me and, if need be, could fit so many people. When various professionals on business trips—veterinarians, tractor drivers, teachers, and engineers—came into town, the collective farm chairman would always have them stay in our house. The clean and bright rooms of the house would open their doors to new visitors time and again... it was a kind house."

The heat of this kindness seemed to warm his heart:

I remember those early days, when father used to live with us... the games we played, our walks through the garden, through the fields... I remember how the pea plants grew, straight out of a fairytale... Nearby there was a big pond with fish."

However, this world was soon split in two. From early on, fear moved into his soul alongside love:

I always felt like there was something I needed to avoid. I felt good with my family, but when strangers came into the house, I acutely felt the need to run away and hide.

It was not merely a matter of the danger that lurked just about everywhere. A "rescued child" is perceptive in sensing their otherness from the world around them. Holidays and celebrations made this sharply apparent:

...So many people gathered in the big dining room, set the table for the feast, sang... Every time I ran away, feeling so lonely that I'd begin to cry. Even the songs they sang seemed foreign to me. I felt there was a big wall separating me from them... On mass public holidays, it was even more intense. I felt myself retreating away from it all... I couldn't explain it to myself. Perhaps something deep inside them, some sort of entirely alien aesthetic wave lifted everyone up, leaving me high and dry.

The "rescued child's" self-reflections submerge us into the depth of human psychology:

There were times when Lithuanian words began sounding completely strange to me. The language, its Samogitian dialect sounded so rough to me.

One word in particular scratched his ears, a word whose meaning he didn't know for a long time:

During recess at school, the kids running past would tease me: yid, yid!

We would be just playing, and then suddenly someone would drop that little word in.

It almost seemed innocent. But I still felt that it was a sign that everyone besides me understood.

Sometimes my playmates would surround me, spelling it out letter by letter: y-i-d. They'd just stand around, repeating it loudly. Moreover, I rarely saw any malice on their faces. But their ostensibly good-natured laughing would still ring in my ears, continuously...

When I was in first grade, a fourth-grader picked me up off my feet one day. For a long time, he carried me across the hall-way, quite gently, I would say. Then he seemed to remember something he had to do — and roughly flung me aside. I fell hard against a bench.

Alfonsas highlights that these were all signals that made his thoughts race. But his thoughts layered up one on top of the other, interrupting one another:

Why do I look nothing like my family? My complexion is dark, theirs are light. And of course, the hair: all of my cousins are blond. Though mom had dark hair, it was not quite the same as mine...

Everything was wrapped in mystery. My childhood was wrapped in mystery like a piece of candy.

I often thought that I appeared in this Lithuanian village by complete accident — unnaturally somehow.

Who was I then? And where did I come from?

I'll say again that I was afraid of this mystery, really didn't want to get too close to it.

Early on, another question came into his mind: who were these Jews everyone was talking about?

The adults—not my parents, of course—would tell jokes about Jews.

They would tell stories that would send a chill through my spine. For example, they would say that Jews drink the blood of Christian babies...

I was seven or eight years old when I realized that I had some sort of connection with the Jews. I got scared. After all, the Jews were bad people: murderers, scalpers... Since then, this fear has not left me. The fear of participating in something dirty and wrong. And a sense of loneliness as a result.

With great pain, he looked for ways out, but found only dead-ends:

Now and then, everything seemed to get far away from me: nature, my family... And it seemed that there was nobody that could help me. Like I had ended up all alone on a tiny island.

The state of his soul was strangely reflected in the world around him:

The feeling that the world was hostile towards me would come to me every time the seasons changed.

I would get weak all of a sudden. The silence would start ringing. And the world once again grew more and more distant.

And I would end up on that small island once again. Utterly alone.

There were also the dreams:

In my dreams I was chased down by animals, by strangers... The horses, their horses galloped behind me.

2

...Bukontas' poems reveal the "story of his soul" just as sharply, albeit in their own way.

He had already grown up and began his studies at Vilnius University, majoring in Lithuanian language and literature. Though the world around him was still cold and strange, his creative pursuits, as always, overcame his loneliness. Had the world shrunk down to the size of that tiny island where the waves of hatred had tossed him? Perhaps it had, which was why Alfonsas was determined to stretch the limits of the earthly, determined to unlock the door to the universe:

> I want to unite
> bird and stone,
> dark and light,
> loss and hope...

Those shores that cannot be brought together

> I want to unite
> beginning and end.
> I made a
> fire in the valley
> after long and heavy rain.
> Have you heard my voice?
> Have seen how the windmills
> of stars were spinning?
> Come down to the little bridge
> I am building for you,
> come, because I must leave.
> With a burning coal
> write my name on the water.

Here, the poet is not just addressing his contemporary, his fellow in the universe. This poem is not merely his creative manifesto. In these verses, I hear the voice of the "rescued child," who has finally stepped onto the path towards spiritual freedom. Like many Jews before him, he began his journey through "the desert."

Naturally, I instantly heard the resonance between the Lithuanian writer and the brilliant American poet Walt Whitman. Bukontas wrote "The Little Bridge" when he was very young. The young poet, following in the footsteps of Whitman, comes face to face with eternity, feeling almost like a demiurge before it. He aimed to discern the cosmos within human souls and see the human soul up among the stars. That's the source of Bukontas' trust to everyone he encounters:

I will take with you along the day where nobody lives anymore. Is there really something that you regret? Do you really want to drop your word on the pavement? Lean on me, lean on me, and look into the void. And now we are both free from our ties, our branches, our trunks—become seed and star. The birds of dawn fly out from our shoulders, from our eyes, from our lips.

Reading these lines, I see a young man from a typical Lithuanian village. A "rescued" Jewish child, attempting to find grounding and roots by himself. Finding grounding and roots in the universe itself. Whitman's *Leaves of Grass* clearly made an impact on him, defining his creative journey. At this point, I can't help but to briefly digress. Back in Soviet times, criticism often had a vulgar take on the problem of literary tradition. Noticing the influence of Mayakovsky on someone's verse, our critics would talk about it as if they were giving the poet a medal. Other traditions were deemed dangerous, detrimental to "artistic growth." At times, the problem of tradition would be reduced to discussions of imitation and emulation. But I firmly believe that (if we are dealing with a genuine talent) the discussion should be about a unity of worldview between artists, about a shared direction of their artistic strivings...

Stepping into the limitlessness of space and time, Bukontas seemed better-equipped than his contemporaries at asking sharp, at times merciless questions. That's when you can fully appreciate the advantages of taking on a "cosmic" perspective! Only on the cosmic level is it suitable to move aside the factors of civilization and culture and genuinely ask yourself: what is a human being? What is our sacred essence? What is our unique mission? Those are topics that Bukontas' poems often explore, including "The Snowman":

I am naked: without age or surname. I try to cover myself up during the day—but in vain: the strike of lightning between the future and the past is my shame. The more you think about it: everyone loses the same thing, the same thing everyone is look-ing for. The truth is walking, leaving bare footprints on the white plain. Who left in a hurry, forgetting to put on their shoes? Whose footprints in the snow are those? Whose footprints on the fearless page?"

You can come to understand the laws of the cosmos in various ways. You can read them in the sacred texts of old. You can discover them for yourself, listening to the rhythms of the universe. The latter route was the one chosen by Bu-kontas' lyric persona. Undoubted he saw the equal splendor of living and non-living nature, the equality of the seemingly mutually exclusive origins of being. Perhaps remembering his childhood, he understood the dangers of giving permanents names—"to coppices, to stones, to the man in the mirror." Perhaps, dividing the whole world up and putting labels on everything are the greatest mistakes we make on our path, the greatest mistakes of humankind:

> It seems that as soon as names return
> we will collide into one another,
> and the endless river will meld with
> the sky along the endless plain.

Bukontas' poetry often records what happens when the eternals laws are broken. In his poem titled "The Song of Horst Wessel" after the Nazi Party anthem, we see a sol-dier blinded by the power of his weapons. Then, "with open mouths they continue the song already below their roots." What's the poem "Monument" about? About defending a dy-ing mother nature? No, it is humanity committing suicide, since we are all "nature" once we transform "into earth, into air, or into the ringing of the river."

An artist's consciousness is not a sponge: it only takes in what it's able and what it needs to take in, only what co-heres with the developmental logic of creative individuality.

I say this having Bukontas' approach to his literary influences and predecessors in mind. For instance, there's Tadeusz Różewicz—Bukontas helped the Lithuanian reader discover his short stories and poems through his translations. Różewicz was firm in his belief that poetry needed to be written out of "nothing," using the simplest of words. Such a creative approach resonated with Bukontas' own. But it was also important for him to look and see what lay behind and beyond the word. To look not so much into the depths of phenomena, events, and action, but into the depth of images and premonitions. This is a typical subject for his poems. One of them is even called "On the other side of words." The poet takes "astonishments" and weaves "a tree, a dream, the heat of touch, a living creature, the tremble of suffering" out of them. I'll note that Sergei Karneev's translation of the poem's final lines are slightly inaccurate:

Bukontas' orginal:

> Your words no longer mean anything...
> Only space and silence...
> Only the flight remains...

Karneev's translation:

> The line of verse is like a landing strip.
> It starts to soar. It flies. Its aim is far away...

"Only the flight remains..." That's what the poet discovers "on the other side of words."

Of course, the cosmic tradition in world poetry doesn't begin with *Leaves of Grass*. Henry David Thoreau remarked while reading Whitman's book "It is strange how similar it is to work of the Indian prophets..." Bukontas himself came to study the Sanskrit tradition. In the 1870s, he became enthralled by the Upanishads. At the time he quit writing original poetry for a long time, a shift noticed by readers and critics alike with great alarm. The shift made sense to me, albeit only retrospectively. In the ancient traditions, when an artist or poet left the world for the monastery, he would take a vow silence, renouncing his craft for decades, if not forever. His purpose in doing this was to intently listening in to his own "I," connect with God, possibly find his own voice at the end of it all.

Granted, in those difficult yet, as it turned out, still quite productive years, Alfonsas Bukontas continued to translate. This choice was not just a serious and important part of Lithuanian cultural production. It was also a choice that often appears to lead to a paradoxical conclusion: by working with another culture, an artist often ends up returning to himself. Translating Pushkin's late philosophical lyrics, his thoughts turned once again to a poet's calling. Aleksandr Blok's cycle dedicated to Carmen drew him in with its musicality, leading him to ask: how would it sound in Lithuanian? In his mother tongue, Bukontas recreated the works of many poets that lived in his home region: the Polish poet Konstanty Gałczyński, the German F. Braun, the Belarusian Maksim Tank, the Crimean Karaite S. Frikovich... I could list many names of authors and titles of works that Bukontas translated, but for now will mention only the sonnets and tercets of the Russian philosopher Lev Karsavin[19]. Karsavin composed these verses not long before his death in the Gulag, quite sure that his voice will be heard beyond the grave. And he was right: Bukontas found Karsavin's works in Vilnius archies.

And naturally he had to translate the works of Karsavin's mental interlocutors — across decades and centuries. These included Nikolai Roerich's long poem[20] "Instruction to the Hunter who Steps into the Forest" and the famous *Bhagavad Gita*. We can read some symbolism into the fact that Bukontas' translation of the *Bhagavad Gita*, a dense tome which condenses all of the Sanskrit teachings that inspired him, ended his period of poetic silence.

3

Let's not forget that a "rescued child" slowly returns to their family. *All this time*, Alfonsas told me, *I felt like I was wandering through the desert. Moreover, my journey lasted longer than forty years, a lot longer. One day I realized that I wouldn't be able to leave the desert if I don't come to understand for myself: why am I being tested?*

The Jewish family, founded by Abraham, is thousands of years old. Perhaps this sounds a little highfalutin, seems like something out of a fairytale? It didn't happen immediately, but Bukontas clearly came to understand the concept of time in Judaism. In the words of the kabbalist Adin Steinsaltz, wiseman of our times, events don't sink in the river of time like stones. They are merely borne away from us by the current."

From hints, slips of the tongue, chance conversations, and sudden confessions, Bukontas was able to reconstruct the story of his rescue, his parents' lives and death—to get closer to them.

Once again, Vaclovas Martinkus, the Catholic priest, was unexpectedly of great help. After the end of the war, he was able to emigrate to the West. He now lived in the US and would sometimes write to his friends back in Lithuania. Martinkus was inquiring about the fate of the child he had helped rescue, then began corresponding with Alfonsas himself. Alas, the KGB intercepted those letters and used them to blackmail Bukontas and his friends. Martinkus sent back various gifts and clothes, told Alfonsas about the town of Židikai, a town with a Jewish population of about 230 before the war, told him about the events of the summer of 1941, when the war broke out. One time, Martinkus was able to save the Jews of Židikai from being executed by demanding the German army officers to show the court decision. A few months later, however, when a different regiment was passing through town, nobody stopped to listen to the priest. They even threatened to executive Martinkus together with the Jews he was trying to save...

(Martinkus also talked about his life nowadays. This was eye-opening for Alfonsas: aside from his religious and philanthropic activities, the priest was a singer-songwriter, traveled a lot, constantly discovering the world and its people. In Israel, for instance, he had a lively discussion with David Ben-Gurion. Martinkus still cared about Alfonsas after all these years: he showed his poems to the literary idol of the Lithuanian émigré community Bernardas Brazdžionis, who praised them highly.)

Time became alive once again: the past, present, and future all existed in a single dimension. The Kabbalah and Roerich's writings both speak of this happening. The Lithuanian painter Mikalojus Čiurlionis[21] was keenly attuned to this feeling. Alfonsas was quite taken by his painting called "The Past," which depicted opening gates, through which shone the sun, or rather multiple suns.

The rays of the past began to warm the "rescued child":

When I was a student, I came to visit my aunt Kotryna Šiulcen, with whom I had lived long ago, back when I was studying in Židikai... We went walking with her through a meadow, and she told me everything she knew. She told me a lot... Even my real name... It turns out that before the war, she was my parents' neighbor, helping my mom run the household. It turns out that my aunt Kotryna was the one who took me to the priest Martinkus' house in Dapšiai...

Alfonsas' story resonated with that of the great Yiddish poet Hirsch Osherovich[22] who lived in Vilnius after the war:

He was also a graduate of Vytautas Magnus University. Osherovich found lawyers, colleagues of his father, and helped me find other people who knew my parents. That's when I learned the details of their final days: they ended up in the Kaunas ghetto; my father was shot in 1942, my mother was taken to Stutthof in 1933. She died in March of 1945 during a prison break from the camps... Father's little brother and sister were killed in a pine forest near Mažeikiai... I held their photographs in my hands, staring in stunned silence. There was my mom (she probably tried to escape Stutthof because she found out, back in the ghet-

to, that I had rescued), and there was my dad, studying at the Sorbonne... there was my brother... was that baby really... me?

The mystery was solved, but the truth was not easy to bear: *I rarely talk to anyone about my past. Sometimes, the other people will ask about it and get frightened: a gaping chasm opens up before them, a chasm they want to quickly get to the other side of... My interlocutor always promptly changes the subject. I understand this response: it's the instinct of self-preservation.*

As if casting off the shrouds of time by truly grasping the chain of events and their meaning, Alfonsas recalls how a "tall bald man in a leather jacket from Kaunas" came to his town in 1947. He had an unusual assignment: finding the "rescued" Jewish children in Lithuanian villages. Rumor was that these boys and girls were later shipped off to Palestine...

The man gave me a piece of candy and gifted me some sort of coin. Mom spoke with him behind closed doors. He spent the night at our place. In the morning I saw him leave by walking through our garden... I felt strange and afraid. I didn't want to leave my home. I was firmly convinced that my home was an old fortress, where I could hide, away from all danger.

It wasn't just the underground post-war Zionist activists that understood the importance for a "rescued child" to find a family. It was also evident to a simple Lithunian peasant woman named Marija Bukontas.

"You already know everything, you're not a child anymore," she told me one day. Then she asked, *"Perhaps I made a mistake by not giving you away to people who were closer related to you by blood?" I was already 19 years old at the time. Yet she was still tortured by her choice, worried that I was left all alone in the world... She cried. I assured her that I was very happy to be living with them, that I was grateful to them for everything... This conversation only happened once. We never returned to the subject again. But it seemed like my mom still thought about it sometimes, wondering if a child of one nationality could be replanted in the family of another. She felt like she had violated some divine laws...*

The broken lines of his fate eventually converged.

On December 22, 1994, the Vilnius court, supported many pieces of evidence and multiple living witnesses, came to the decision that Alfonsas Bukontas was actually Mordecai Mikhnitsky, son of Nehama Gurvičiate-Mikhnitsky (1907–1945) and Jankelis Mikhnitsky (1907–1942).

4

...I hope to one day publish an account of Alfonsas' return to his true home. Here I have given only fragments. But here's one more. This is the very beginning of Bukontas' confession — a short novella I would title (for myself at least) "Soft L." This novella is full of loneliness, anguish, anticipation, defined by a yet vague longing to solve the mystery of one's own fate.

...When I started first grade, I met a boy who lived in the house next door to mine.

He was taller and bigger than me. His name was Alfredas.

I can still remember how strangely he'd pronounce his own name, or rather one of its letters — the L... It was soft, far too soft and palatized. Nobody in our village pronounced it like that. And the whole class made fun of him for it!

Everyday Alfredas and I would walk back from school together. Our walk was long: a narrow, seemingly endless path, then a bridge over a stream, then the path again...

There was no one around us for miles.

We slowly became friends; we didn't really have a choice. We even started coming over to each other's homes.

Alfredas had moved to our village not too long again. He had come here from Konigsberg. That city had been heavily bombed during the war. If I am not mistaken, his parents had during the bombing. Many children had fled from Konigsberg, often escaping on train car roofs. They would wander around the villages, begging for change. They quickly picked up some key Lithuanian words: dúonas (bread), valgyti (eat)... But it was easy to tell that they were German.

Our neighbor was a lawyer in the regional office. Once he spotted Alfredas and took a liking to the boy. The man's only daughter had died, so he offered to let Alfredas live with his family. Soon after they officially adopted the boy and gave him a Lithuanian surname.

Alfredas loved to draw airplanes and tanks all the time. In general, all of his games were somehow war-themed. One time he told me that his real dad had been a pilot.

Half a year later, Alfredas was already fluent in Lithuanian.

But strangely enough, his "soft l" never fully went away.

Alfredas and I went to the same school for seven years. And the whole time we felt alienated from the people around us.

Indeed, Alfredas and I were strangers here. Though it was difficult to say what exactly made us stand out. Moreover, the two of us were nothing alike.

Alfredas was very strong. He would get into fights whenever he felt the hostility of his environment.

Being weak, I avoided fights at all costs...

When the brawls ended, Alfredas and I would walk back home like nothing had happened. The tension seemed to subside. But our reality remained torn asunder, doubled... And that, strangely enough, was what united us.

Our teacher would tell the parents at the school with a didactic tone in her voice, "You see, the Jewish boy and the German boy get along, but we can't seem to follow their lead..."

I only recently learned that she had said that. I hadn't a clue back then that I was Jewish. Perhaps, on a subconscious level, I didn't want to know it.

...Naturally, I would often wonder why Alfonsas began his confession with a story about his childhood friend.

In another's fate, he had seen his own reflection, as in a mirror. But in essence they had only one point of commonality: Alfredas and Alfonsas were othered in their small Lithuanian village.

Bukontas later came to the conclusion that every person has their own path, their purpose. And some people's purpose was to serve as a bridge between different nationalities and cultures.

5

...A "rescued child's" return to their past isn't always idyllic. Trying to find a Jewish community as a young man, Alfonsas felt insecure at times: "...my new acquaintances would laugh at what I had to say, like the kids in the village before them." Of course, he had idealized Jews in his mind and was shocked: was it really possible that his fellow descendants of Abraham had a sort of national apathy, cynicism, and indifference to the suffering of others? The situation that the young writer had gotten himself into, however, was every more dramatic:

At a certain point, it seemed that I had become a stranger in that culture that seemed like home since childhood. It was very difficult for me to reconnect with my roots, to enter a culture that was mine by blood.

Alfonsas and I talked about this a lot. I remembered my own words from the early 80s, when I was working on a book about Kristijonas Donelaitis, the founder of Lithuanian literature: "Different cultures have different roots, but they all share the same sky." Life, however, is more complicated than any formula. As I see it, Bukontas was able to reconnect with his roots because he was able to get a feel for the *air* of Jewish history and bravely enter into its *special sense of time.*

"...The river of history forms a ring," Adin Steinsaltz writes, "It flows into itself, and in its waters, we will never perceive either irreversible changes or any novelty." But in Judaism eternal return is our perpetual renewal. "Take, for example, the Exodus from Egypt," Steinsaltz continues, "Its meaning goes beyond the mere historical, for it is realized in the spiritual biography of our person. A Jew of any generation not only has to believe that they themselves escaped from Egypt. The story of Exodus becomes the story of their own spiritual development. Slavery and the escape from slavery, the crossing of the Red Sea, the war with Amalekites and the receiving of the Torah—these are all stages in the development of an individual personality."

The path of a "rescued child" is a version of our eternal return...

But naturally, Bukontas didn't negate his past: decades of his life cannot be simply tossed aside like a useless draft. Moreover, for Jews the past organically merges with the present. Alfonsas confessed: *mom and dad came to me out of the void and supported me through my journey, filling the emptiness of my soul I had felt for a long time.* That's why he still *whispers the name of his adopted parents like a prayer, along with the names of his other saviors.*

Bukontas didn't reject his own literary experiments and investigations. No, it was no coincidence that they resonated with his newly found godly soul: he easily found the "cosmic" origins he was seeking in the Torah... And a further proof of how organically he had entered into *a culture he was close to genetically* were, as always, Alfonsas' translations.

From Yiddish, Hebrew, and Russian he translated the works of Jewish poets, one starkly different from another: Joshua Latzman, Hirsh Osherovich, Moshe Kulbak, Abraham Sutzkever, Shmuel Kacherginsky, Herman Kruk, Yehuda Amihai, Leonid Shkolnik, Efrem Bauh (his poetry as well as his novel *The Sun of Suicides*)... Once more he confirmed for himself the ancient truth: a Jewish writer's homeland is our history. The Creator lives in history, but then dissolves within it once and for all.

6

...This is where we must bid farewell to our protagonist, leaving much out of our account. I am not writing a "life and works" account of Alfonsans Bukontas the poet; I am observing his "journey through the desert."

I'll admit that in thinking about my friend's fate, I often return to the line that remain key to understanding him (no wonder it was chosen as the title of the only collection of his works published in Moscow in 1990, translated from the Lithuanian by Sergei Karneev): "while the arrow flies."

The author is engaged in a subtle polemic with Osip Mandelstam's famous poem "Shell."[23] The argument, once again, is about defining a human being. The position on the human that Mandelstam's poem so strikingly takes in 1911 has become widespread in Western art in the second half of the 20th century. Many have demonstrated how a human being is but a lonely speck of sand in the winds of time, a mere (in Mandelstam's words) "useless shell" borne "from the universal deep" onto the shore of life. It seems that the last century seems to fully confirm this position: destines, lives, loves, hopes, emerging and not yet blossomed talents have all been mercilessly destroyed and marred by revolutions, dictatorships, and wars... But Alfonsas Bukontas disagrees:

> No, the shell isn't lost: it cries,
> begging the tide
> to bring it back to the deep. It is barren.
> Only specks of sand
> are whirring within. Returning back is all that remains,
> memory calls it back...
> You are family! You are an arrow
> that has pierced through time!
> The ringing of the drawn bowstring rebels
> within you.

Need I add anything to these words? Only a quote from the Torah can stand beside them: we are one family, and each is responsible for each. Only from the Holy Scripture of Agni Yoga: "Success will never leave those who aim, for it is difficult to land on an arrow in flight."

Emigration as a Dream

Barely awake, I count the days. August — five, September — thirty... This arithmetic gets old by the second month. I start counting weeks. Isn't that the way time is counted for kids — the not-yet- and just-recently-born? In four days, our three month "anniversary" of coming to Chicago. Still trying to figure out — is that considered a long time? (November 1996)

* * *

The pain is persistent. It comes back like contractions, bears in, gives no respite. Sometimes I just want to sink into it, adapt myself, go numb. But I can't. Of course, the pain is present in the night, but it feels farther away as I sleep. This pain has defined the month that I bid farewell to Lithuania and the month and a half I've spent in Chicago. The paramedics in Vilnius tried to help me, to no avail. In the States, generic painkillers from Walgreens finally beat the pain. As the wisemen say: The Almighty warns us through the language of pain.

* * *

The commonplace dimension of immigration is the English language. Our life is with it — and within it.

My English teacher is a Pole. He came to America as a child. Now he's thirty-seven. How do I know this? He told me himself. He also told me:

- *about his wife, five years younger than him, a doctor, who earns three times M's salary. A point of pride.*

126

- *about his lovers, "gyorlfrends," before he got married, his wife had been one of them for a few years.*
- *about his wife's likes and dislikes—she hates bad breath the most, loves to "make love"*
- *the reasons they fight; a common one: when M goes pee pee in the bathroom (the teacher says this in Russian), he lifts the seat up to avoid splash back; the wife comes home from work, hurriedly sits down directly on the cold bowl, jumps up, screams...*

Sometimes I wonder: does M even have a wife? What if all of this is just a pedagogical technique to activate my understanding of his perfect English?

He sits in the middle of the room, legs stretched out. Without pausing his story, he can tie his shoelaces or scratch any part of his seal-like body in front of the whole class. As he talks, he checks the time inconspicuously. I checked many times: never a minute late, he cuts himself off, exactly at three:

"Break."

No, he doesn't half-ass his job—he's a true virtuoso. And, like any master of his craft, he enjoys when I tell him so.

"Oh, really?" M's false modesty.

His virtuosity was on full display at the start of the lesson. He sang songs, acts out different animals, different kinds of Americans... it would seem that M is also a virtuoso at hiding his perfect Russian.

Normally there are about ten or twelve people in the class. The desks were placed in a semi-circle. No textbooks, no grammar. Every day M. would pass around photocopied handouts. These were prompts. Imagine that you're a banker, deciding who to grant a loan to. Or a committee member, deciding, which school programs to cut, which to keep. Or... the handouts were raw data. "We'll discuss tomorrow."

At quarter-to-five sharp, M. shuts his mouth and leaves the room. On a cold day, he throws a brightly colored sweater over his shoulders. Just a short trip to his Toyota Camry in the parking lot.

I'll never know where he would drive off to. (January 1997)

* * *

"Interlude." That's the name of a Yuri Tynianov[24] essay about Russian poetry in the 1920s. "Interlude"—I can't think of a better description for emigration. An emigrant is a man in an interlude.

* * *

Emigration or immigration? A useless debate. Any encyclopedia will tell you: an emigrant is someone who leaves their homeland; an immigrant—someone who moves to a different country. Why am I so interested in emigrants? Their fates inevitable harbor tragedy, or at least a melodrama. They've left Russia (or any other former Soviet republic) but haven't made it to America. They are in an interlude. Forever?

* * *

Emigrants themselves worry about justifying their emigration. They have used many different justifications over the years. Nowadays they typically address the "upper" as opposed to the "lower" person. No one will say or even think to themselves: "We are in exile; we are on a mission." One Chicago journalist in the early 2000s put it a lot more believably, with artless cynicism: "Take a piece of fresh Borodino bread, spread some Vologoda butter on it, and stick a slice of Doktorskaya ham on top... you haven't forgotten your nostalgia for your homeland, have you?" (August 2005)

* * *

The great "truth-seeker" Georgy Gurdzhiev[25] was certain: man is a machine. A being that lives mechanically but is submerged in the narcotic of dreams. Gurdzhiev's experiments, dazzling and charming European intellectuals, pursued a single goal: awakening man from his "daytime dream."

Of course, emigration wakes up our sleeping conscience. I'll say! In the words of Dina Rubina[26], who never exaggerates, to emigrate "is to perform seppuku. And your guts plop down on the sidewalk."

But emigration itself is also a dream.

* * *

Scientists happily declare: "Moving improves your memory. Over the course of their lives, people move an average of five times. Research shows that this is a difficult experience, even more difficult than divorce. However, scientists at the University of New Hampshire have found that moving has at least one upside. It helps you remember what has happened." (News agency in August 2016)

* * *

...As if disputing these scientific conclusions, an odd couple is slowly walking towards me on Devon Avenue. She is tall and lean, like a tree that has lost its leaves to fall. He is portly, unnaturally red-cheeked, barely reaching her shoulder. When they notice me from afar, they smile. Last fall in Hot Springs, Arkansas, we would go for frequent walks in the park, which seemed to hang over the city. Yuri had taught at university like me—fans would come into town just to hear his lectures. Now he was shy and silent. The longest thing he had ever said to me, when we had just met, was: "You can call me by my first name, after all, we met in the West, where people don't use patronymics, isn't that so?"

It took me a while to realize that Alzheimer's had taken him a while ago. But he and his wife hid this fact masterfully. Fira would answer my questions about literature departments in Moldavia. Yuri would sadly and gently nod along.

Once when he dozed off on a park bench, drunk off the crisp mountain air, Fira told me their story in a whisper. Alzheimer's attacked her husband out of the blue and crushed him swiftly. *Thank God we were already here in Chicago, where the future isn't so scary. Thank God that he didn't get aggressive as the doctor had warned. Thank God Yurochka didn't lose his intellect completely.* And he even came up with an explanation for his memory loss: "The majority of writers, bringing up the past, enliven it, take pleasure in remembering. But I don't want to remember. My past is soaked in sorrow."

* * *

"Emigration is an illness," I write in a notepad. And I forget about the most important thing: how long does the illness last? Of course, there are a couple options. Reading Frederick Perls, the founder of gestalt therapy, I come across his reminder: illness is an unresolved situation; it "can resolve through recovery, death or the restructuring of the organism."

* * *

Russophone communities in American cities become havens for the old. Mass emigration from Russia ended long ago. The old arguments in newspapers and on the radio are over: how many KGB agents came along with us? who really wrote *Quietly Flows the Don*? was Georgy Zhukov Russia's savior or a butcher, heartlessly sending soldier to their deaths? Yesterday's debaters, who couldn't stand one another, now peacefully meet at the urologist's office, on a cruise to the Bahamas, or at an old folks' home. (December 2017)

* * *

Human destinies, submerged in the everyday, are revealed in emigration. Emigration highlights their brokenness, their strangeness, oftentimes their mystery.

* * *

On the very same Devon Avenue, the Chicago haven for Russian emigres for many years, stands a man, pressed up to the wall of a grocery store. His appearance at once repels and attracts passersby. About himself he reports: I work as a beggar. It's hard to tell how old he is: somewhere between forty and sixty. In any case, I haven't seen any gray in his ragged bluish beard. He's got a prosthetic left leg, not covered by jeans as is often the case. His most notable feature are his eyes: big or at least they seem to be as he looks at you hard, intently, never averting his gaze.

We hadn't said a word to one another all these years. But I know his name: Ilyusha. A soft, warm name, as if poorly chosen for hire. Many American beggars hold out a can or a box with dollars, the clinking of coins reproaching passersby. But legless Ilyusha looks straight at you, piercing you with his gaze, and you take your wallet out without invitation.

One winter I saw Ilyusha at the doctor's office. He recognized me as he was leaving and stopped. Confidently he asked, "Give me a lift to work?" It's only a five-minute drive, but walking is hard for Ilyusha: the wind in a Chicago winter stings and knocks over even the healthy. In the car he sits in silence, looking out the window—as if seeing the street he had spent decades walking for the first time. Of course, Ilyusha wrinkles his nose at the bad smell from the gray coat he wears in any weather.

We got to talking: at some point he graduated from Moscow State University with a degree in philosophy. Philosophy? I raise a mental eyebrow. And I'm brought back to sentimental 19th-century novels. I don't doubt this legend of émigré life, the kind that gets made into myth. But then T, who knows everything about everyone, swears that he really saw Ilyusha's diploma from Moscow State.

What brought him to Chicago and made him choose this ancient profession? I tried striking up a conversation with Ilyusha many times. But each time he would shove me away with his stare, closing like a bolt in the door.

* * *

Anatoly Simonovich Lieberman[27], famous linguist, professor at the University of Minnesota, tells me on the phone:

"Our Soviet life averaged us out to a shocking extent. Generations like peas in a pod. As my wife would say, like a fireman's gray pants. We recognize each other instantly. All the same quotes, thoughts, memories."

And it's true: I recognize my people everywhere. I recognize my own fear in them without fail: most of us try to hide it. It's the only piece of baggage that, alas, an emigrant can't lose or leave in storage at the airport.

Fear is one of the main themes of my book *Long Conversations in Anticipation of a Joyous Death* (1996). For five years I had listened to the confession of a dying Lithuanian Jewish dramaturg and critic named y. These five years spent "on the very edge of life," y and I try to reconstruct his many fears and deal with them at long last. It just so happened that these fears found their resolution only in his death.

* * *

The day before yesterday after work I'm taking for a walk in the park near my house, talking on the phone. Suddenly— I hear a voice with a strong accent: "How nice—such beautiful Russian..." An older woman. I ask her: "Are you from Russia?" "No, from Latvia. I've been here almost 30 years. And I miss Russian terribly..."?! "I really love learning languages. I know five already, now I'm learning my sixth—Japanese... I'm going to Japan soon for work placement." She tells me about herself some more. Nothing particularly notable, I can't quite figure out what she does for a living (something to do with non-traditional medicine) ...We part ways after a few minutes. She asks to exchange phone numbers.

And soon she actually calls me, "I have a favor to ask of you. If we accidentally meet in some public place, pretend that you don't know me..." She repeats this a few times. I calm her down, give her my word to keep quiet, don't question anything she says. I don't want to get deep *inside* her fears.

* * *

At one point I started recording the dreams of Jews. I began from the Exodus from the country of the red pharaohs. A million people disappeared, as if they had evaporated in history and time. I thought: it was through dreams that I could understand the tragic and tangled history of the Soviet Jewry. No matter how many times we tried to read it today, much remains only a conjecture. Maybe our dreams, I thought, could clarify something. Something that people couldn't talk about before. Something they had already forgotten. And something that they hide to this day — even from themselves (some of these notes made into my book *Aftertaste of a Dream*, 2012).

What about the dreams of emigrants? Here are the ones that repeat, the ones that psychologists assure us are the most important: "We're sitting in an airplane, just touched down in New York. The adults are disgruntled, the children are crying. Finally, thank God, everything got resolved." About ten people have told me this exact "nightmare" with only slight variations.

* * *

An interview with some emigrants-insomniacs: you wake up at 3 am and can't fall back asleep until the morning. They say that at these times the heavens are trying to tell you something important.

Another typical answer: "I love lying in the dark with my eyes closed. I'm trying to see myself from the outside. For years I've been treating myself as a stranger. I ask myself: is there some purpose to this person's life? Is this his fate?"

* * *

I've been editing a Russophone monthly publication in Chicago for more than twenty years. There is no shortage of these kinds of publications in the States: something between a newspaper and a journal. I could write a book about "my time as editor." It's a shame that this book already exists (see Mark Twain's notes or the novellas of Dina Rubina).

* * *

Emails from William F. are full of surprises. He is also a "philosopher," one of the many "philosophers" of the Russophone community. His ideas always shock me. Here's his missive from today, which he clearly wrote to provoke a response from the editors:

"It is known that there are many lesbians and homosexuals in our society. Typically, they don't have kids. However, you shouldn't mismanage your own biological material. Why shouldn't we support bisexuals impregnating lesbians? That way these women would achieve harmony in their lives. And we'll be sure to get major population growth. Indeed, homosexuals need to be slowly, but surely—with the help of scientific advancements—be led into the ranks of bisexuals." (6 November 2017)

* * *

In the new edition of Yuri Olesha's diaries[28] , which was previously called *Not Day Without a Line*, now reedited and expanded as *The Book of Farewell*, I read: "Human fate, lonely human fate [...] is an avoidable subject for generations. Works of world literature are based upon it. The best thing written about this in the last few years—Remarque's book. It somehow echoes with a different book of solitary human fate—Hamsun's "Hunger." Now I turn to my own fate and I see loneliness. In this epoch of mass movements let there be a book about loneliness.

Loneliness, like falseness, is the symbol of emigration. (August 2000)

* * *

I come into the editorial office at different times—at 9, 10, 11 am. There's no rush: I could work from home. But Boris is sitting in the waiting room, restless. I'm ashamed, I apologize profusely before him every time. But what's there to apologize for: in America you set up a meeting beforehand, no one "drops in" like in Russia.

"What's new?" I ask, though I already know his response, "Sorry, I don't get enough communication." Boris is a pretty good poet. I ask him to read me his old poems, ask him about

Tadjikistan, where he lived and was published some time ago. What else can I do for him?

* * *

These old emigrants (eighty and over) are the typical Soviet crowd. They rarely come to insight like Boris, who concludes his letter with a sigh: "Communism is a wonderful idea! We just have to make sure it never comes true."

* * *

Another point of discussion about emigration: "Are you happy in the US?" Svetlana P is indignant: "I didn't come here and learn English just to clean other people's home..." Inna M responds, "Svetlana would be right, of course, if she didn't speak English like so many of our old folks: Yours mine yesterday coming..."

We love to overestimate *our own*.

* * *

Books rush into the publishing house on a stream. I'm often puzzled: why do so many, having just emigrated, want to become writers? And—immediately pick up "quill and ink," that is to say they learn how to work the computer.

Here they lose their profession (typically, it's become redundant). But in their soul they feel the an unshakable urge: I have a unique life experience, I absolutely must talk about it.

Alas, writing books is also a profession. 99.9% of books written in emigration are the colorless products of graphomania.

* * *

Emigration as an idea and as a reality are two different things.

As an idea, emigration is wonderful: it shows the writer the essence of many things, especially his true calling.

Alas, the reality of emigration is different. Crude. Cynical. Harsh. All highlighting the uselessness of creative work.

* * *

The Russian writer, of course, is among the emigrants. It makes no difference if he knows English. He thinks and writes in Russian.

He is in the interlude. Isn't that why so many writers in emigration are overwhelmed by anxiety and frustration? Frustration with whom? With Russia, where they weren't appreciated and even now the critics don't notice them. With anti-Semites (back in Russia, though there's no state anti-Semitism there anymore). With American bureaucrats. And of course, with themselves. With their own fate. Sooner or later, they understand the purposelessness of this feeling. Is it submission or are they only pretending?

The essence of this feeling was formulated by Fritz Perls: anxiety is the rupture, the tension between "now" and "then."

* * *

The talented poetess Anna B. passed away. Her articles about émigré writers are full of spite. Hypocrisy? How did she not understand that? Of course, she understood. But it was too late. On her death bed, she would call up the people that just recently she had doused with buckets of bile. Now she asked for their forgiveness.

* * *

"Hello, brother, it is very hard to write!" the Serapion brothers would say to one another. In emigration, this greeting comes off mocking: who's going to hear the lonely voice of the author, trying to say something in a foreign language?

Still emigration is the best place for creative work. That is to say if you're able to rein in your irrepressible vanity.

* * *

In November 2013 an old doctor died in Chicago, an emigrant from Ukraine Roman Vershgub[29]. So many people take a secret with themselves when they die. I always thought that there's no need to try to figure it out — everyone has the right to leave some act in your life-plot unspoken. But nevertheless, this was a special case.

I heard that Roman Vershgub writes short stories from Efim Petrovich Chepovetsky[30] , the famous children's poet, who had spent his last years living in Chicago.

"Remarkable prose," Efim exclaimed, "The only issue is that Roman doesn't want to publish any of it."

He typed out his stories on a typewriter, making two-three copies. And he gave them to two-three people to read. When we met, Roman granted me this honor. What grabbed me about his stories? They were clearly written by a professional.

I made the same mistake as the others. I asked him, I can recommend your works to one of the émigré journals that I'm a part of, if you want? He gave a hard pass.

He was already hopelessly sick by then, and he knew that. So eventually he caved to his friends and started reading his stories in Chepovetsky's literary studio. However, he was even more adamant in his belief in the uselessness of publication.

Maya, Roman's widow, went against his wishes. I can't criticize her though. In the past legends about Maya the homeopath would travel around Kyiv. Now, a few decades later, she did Western gymnastics, drove a car. She came into my publishing house a few times. She was looking for advice: how do I make the collection? What should I call the book? And the most important thing: how do I interpret the subtext of this or that short story.

She was troubled by the mystery of her husband. Roman never let his wife read his prose. Was he shy, knowing her good taste and harsh judgments? Maybe. Did he not trust her? Doubtful. There was point denying: he loved Maya and was dedicated to her for the many years of their marriage.

I had collected a big folder of Vershgub's stories. Sometimes I look them over. These are sad stories, entirely cheerless at first glance. One of them has following epigraph: "Successes are illusory, troubles are real." The hero of this novella is a young scientist named Vitaly, who deserves the title of genius. All of a sudden, he abandons his dissertation at the defense, leaves his parent's home—moves in with an unattractive woman, a lot older than him ("mama's boy"). Sasha the surgeon who performs impossible procedures suddenly loses his touch and desperately tries to figure out, who's fault is it—is it really him? ("made his own luck"). "I recognize real events and real people in his stories," Maya tells me. And finally, I get it: the space of R.V. stories is a kind of psychoanalytic laboratory. Here he as someone who doesn't believe in God but trusts fate aims to get into logic and meaning, or that the illogic and meaninglessness of being.

In early April I bumped into Maya on the same Devon Avenue. We hurriedly exchanged new. "Did you get the book?" "Not yet. It came out already? Congratulations! How many copies?" "Fifty." "That's so few..." "It's a lot. Thirty books are lying around in the closet—nobody needs them."

Maya sighed: "Up there, in the sky, Roman is judging me, of course..."

* * *

In the US there are more than two million registered authors. Sometimes thinking about this makes me not want to write. I imagine the competition between two million ants.

* * *

But still, to defend creative work. Man was made in God's image. How's that relevant? Man was—first and foremost—created by a demiurge. Creativity helps the emigrant to keep within himself a thin, constantly shrinking layer of spirituality.

* * *

The tragedy of emigration: it gives freedom; however, frequently it closes the world off instead of opening it up.

"What should I do with my freedom?" The same Efim Petrovich Chepovetsky asks me this. He's over ninety years old. But he still writes, loves getting together. At one point his poetry was praised by Samuil Marshak, Lev Kassil',

Mikhail Svetlov. Millions of children would read his books, their names spring to mind: "Mytsik the Mouse," "Fidget, Crumbling, and Notso," "About the Great Queen Nasturtium Petrovna," "The Soldier Peshkin and company" ...I met Chepovetsky more than 40 years ago, when I wrote my first book about the "school of Vsevolod Ivanov." This trailblazer of the Russian avant-garde of the 1920s, the oppositional classical author of Soviet literature taught young writers first and foremost about artistic searching, constant doubt, which is so important in art. In February 1972 I published previously unknown reviews of Ivanov about the "younger generation" in *Literaturnaya gazeta*. The most interesting review was dedicated to the work of Efim Chepovetsky. Now, forty years later, EP persistently keeps on asking me: "So what do I do with my freedom?"

* * *

Mikhail K died — a somber man. He helped so many and never expected thanks in return. And it seems like he never got it. No one really knew his life story. M himself would tell me: during the war he was in recon, ended in the camps (in Stalin's). After being released, he quickly tried to compensate for what he had missed, went to university, quickly defended his dissertation, became famous for his inventions, which was the reason they didn't let him out into the West for so long. As he was telling me his story, one minor detail bothered me: at the start of the war M was very young, but still he managed — all so quickly? — to get the rank of colonel, which he didn't get back after his rehabilitation. MK's American fate was obvious: he became a university professor, had his own grad students, started his own company.

In his huge apartment, filled with antiques, M looks like a weary traveler who accidently stumbled into an expensive hotel. As if nonchalantly, without giving much meaning to his confession, he remarks, "I have no one to talk to. I don't watch TV. I only get the news from the papers. Everything is clear to me anyway."

Three times a week, without fail, M visited the nursing home, one of these days, the oncology division of Lutheran General Hospital. He told me about his visits, unperturbed and precise as always, "They're just lying there, nobody needs them, their kids have forgotten them. My only comfort is that they would be a lot worse off back in Russia"; "When they need me, I translate from English, Russian, Yiddish…"; "I always read them Scripture. They listen intently, though they probably don't understand much."

M had his own relationship with the Bible. He was always unafraid and unequivocal:

"The Torah was given to us by aliens. Every reasonable person knows this. Aliens are the representatives of High reason. They are the ones who gave Earth moral laws for humans to live by. How could it be otherwise?"

He would look at me inquisitively, with a mischievous glint in his eyes, as if inviting a discussion about the Revelation at Sinai. Of course, I didn't try to argue with MK.

* * *

My oldest friend, the wonderful writer Vladimir Ilyich Porudominsky tells me about Cologne, where he's been living for 11 years: "I like it here, but this city will be never become my past. It doesn't grow on me, only off me." Vladimir left Moscow for Germany, following the families of his two daughters. He left the same room he was born in 77 years ago. (May 15, 2005)

* * *

September 11, 2001. Las Vegas. We were going to meet up with my university friend Emil Gorshteyn and his wife Dina. The night before, September 10th—a wonderful evening, the four of us. In the morning—a call from Emil: "Turn on the TV."

I saw the Twin Towers fall in New York, thinking to myself: what is this? Is this really the end of civilization?

Walking out of our hotel room, we walk through the casino hall. There—everywhere—huge TV screens that no one is paying attention to. The game goes on. (September 18, 2001)

* * *

"...So, a waking dream," I ask again, happy that I have solved the riddle of emigration, "What is that?"

Efraim B. gives an inspired speech about the *galut*. The exile of the Jews for thousands of years, which our wisemen call a *dream*.

* * *

"When will the Lord return the children of Sinai from captivity, [all that has happened] will appear to be a dream." *This was the song sung to the Levites as they stood at the steps of the Temple.*

* * *

Why is the *galut* a dream? Contradictory phenomena come together here. Lies suddenly take the form of truth. Reason is eclipsed (the Hassidim believe that this is a dream too).

Georgy Gurdzhuev spent long years thinking about this, persistently trying to convince his students of this truth that was so apparent to him.

* * *

It turns out that my notebooks have long been filled with waking dreams, or people from dreams, to be precise.

* * *

The professions emigrants take up are surprising. Moti Sh. Tells me about his friend Borya (another undocumented immigrant, just left Chicago for New York):

"What do you think, what kind of jobs did they offer to Borya? Selling shoes for dogs! Not in some small shop, mind you, but on a big plaza..."

Moti is Israeli. Shaved head, blue, mischievous eyes. I think he's impossible to confuse, though Moti often tries to confuse the people he's speaking to with the shameless look in his eyes. He was born and went to school in Moscow, moved to Israel, got his bachelor's at the Hebrew University of Jerusalem in political science, speaks three languages—Russian, Hebrew, and English. He became undocumented in Chicago after his student visa application got rejected. His life consists of his neglected apartment, a few neighbors, roommates, random side-jobs. Why doesn't he go to Israel or Russia? Moti won't answer this question. He likes this condition of eternal indeterminacy, of complete openness to fate. Moti talks about his last job with gusto. He drives around a doctor who makes house visits to the elders (this isn't really a common thing in the US). While the doctor is talking to his patient, Moti lounges in his car, smiling at his own thoughts, mentally shuffling his options for the future.

* * *

I call him up and—he comes over. Calm, serious. He paces my apartment with a tape measure and calculator. He's not worried about the particularities of our refurbishments: my wife and I want to paint the walls and the ceilings, but instead, crushed by fatigue, decide not to move the cabinets, nor to take the books off the shelves, nor to put dishes and papers away in boxes. "Let's call it a cosmetic refurbishing," says Sergei with a smile, understanding everything. He talks to me without fawning, but also without that barely concealed boorishness, the sin of many Russian handymen. He names a price a bit higher than what I was planning on paying. But I don't argue with him, I'm already sure: he's our guy, he's one of our own.

Sergei works quietly, rarely asking me questions. I'm sitting with my laptop in the kitchen, which was painted last year, making the next edition of the journal. At midday I find the lunch my wife made in the fridge and invite Sergei to join me at the table. He declines and takes his own food out of his blue bag. He does agree to join me for tea with candies. At tea, he calmly tells me that he's in the country illegally. Of course, I get the logic of his bravery: in America no one is going to arrest you for confessing this to them, at least not yet, and perhaps I could help him.

I look Sergei over furtively, doing the mental math: he's 35, he's spent 8 years in Chicago. His hair is the color of wheat, always neatly cut; his eyes small, but always warm, tiger-colored. He has a straight nose, big hands, which, I have come to believe, are capable of doing anything. His clothes aren't quite working-class, he dresses as if he's counting on being seen by someone whose opinion means a lot to him: his jeans, his gray flannel shirt have been fitted to his form. It's amazing how put together, elegant even Sergei remains by the end of the day.

What's so magnetizing about him for me? It's his calmness, or more accurately his feeling of freedom, which I can't quite understand. It would seem that Sergei has to hurry back to Russia, hurry to live his life, not just get ready for it. His wife Anya, kids — a boy and a girl — are back in the suburbs of Tambov. He's got no future in America, and yet he's still breathing easy. He sends money through Western Union once a month and shows me a photo of a two-story house, built on his blueprint. And is completely silent about leaving.

Sometimes I really want to see Sergei. I am able to find reasons. The door to the entranceway closet breaks, a rocking chair made in China breaks into pieces. He fixes everything well and quickly. Then we eat breakfast (or lunch) and talk *life*. Sergei refuses to take my money. We're mates now, if not bosom friends. But I always make sure to sneak a few bills into his coat pocket as he leaves. And he accepts, defeated by my reasoning: "If you don't accept, I won't be able to call you up the next time."

Of course, soon I learn the reason behind his illogical optimism. "I have to introduce to Rita sometime," say Sergei. They both live in the so-called Ukrainian Village in a house with four apartments. Each has their own apartment to be sure, but they're together. Six years already. No more about Rita. Though Sergei tells me about his communes of undocumented immigrants. "I'm something like their village elder." I'm quick to imagine their frequent parties, night and day ("we're around fifteen"), their unsentimental care for one another, which keeps them alive: undocumented immigrants, for example, have a tough time accessing health care. Their sad farewell: now and again someone books a one-way ticket, though they can't imagine life outside this strange wilderness.

* * *

"What do you do on Sundays?" I ask him once, when Sergei comes on a Monday. Somehow, I get the feeling that he wanted me to ask him this.

Nevertheless, he's embarrassed, he even blushes: "We spend the whole day in bed. And we don't get tired at all." His eyes light up—a typical, funny kind of masculine pride. "And you know sometimes when I wake up I forget where I am. And then I think that we are still in our village, that first happy year after my marriage to my wife."

* * *

I never ended up meeting Rita. I catch a glimpse of her in August in a video on Sergei's phone. She'll tell him about leaving the day before her flight. "She couldn't do it earlier. She hadn't made up her mind. And I don't blame her. Her eldest son is getting married in Kaliningrad." She gets on board the plane without looking back. Petite, as if frozen, in a fashionable summer outfit, very attractive even in her hopeless despair. (December 2016)

* * *

The joy of oblivion. The topic of an essay that I've been trying to write for years before I realize that this thought has become obvious to everyone.

As everyone knows, the acceptance of death, confirmation of it is one of the stages on man's final journey. But it turns out that it's possible to accept one's own oblivion just as peacefully. And even achieve a joyful state.

...On Thursday Yura and Fira come to visit me. They are flustered and calm—all at once. They want to tell me about a recent, unusual decision of theirs. "You know," says Fira, "in the late 70s the KGB would bring Yurocka in for questioning. Yes, as an anti-Soviet dissident. Then everything seemed to quiet down and fall into place. But so many of Yurochka's manuscripts that were seized by the authorities, and we never got them back. So imagine: just recently a young researcher from Moldovia got in contact with us. And told us the most unbelievable news! He found one of Yura's plays in the archives of the KGB. What play, you ask? Scenes from life in Ancient Rome. But it's full of allusions to contemporary issues, like all liberal literature of the time. *The play's a work of genius! the young man tells us on the phone, You must publish it!* And he seemed to have already gotten in touch with a press that was compiling a volume. We're completely flustered. Yurochka is adamant that he's never written a play in his life. I wasn't with him back then. Maybe there's been some kind of mistake? Maybe it's KGB setup? In any case, we decided to decline the offer to publish. Why? Would it have even change our lives?"

From my window I can see them walking on Devon Avenue, not in a hurry as always. Yura, as if he's a child again, is afraid to let go of his wife's hand. And the great joy of oblivion, consciously chosen and accepted within their souls, makes them happy.

* * *

So many resent that profane banality that is ever-present in emigration. But this banality is its only unshifting ground.

* * *

A Russian restaurant with a characteristically pretentious name "Zhivago" was set up near a graveyard. The restaurant is always full of costumers: after funerals people come here — *to commemorate.* I like that. Remembering the dead, you think of yourself, of course. Your life is short, my dear. What have you done, what have you accomplished? You've tried to get ahead, lied your way through. You've buried your talent so deep that you won't find it. Ahead of you, ahead of everyone is a hole in the ground, surrounded by cement tiles. But a foul joy defeats all of these thoughts with a shot of vodka: you're still alive, alive!

* * *

I always feel bad for Russian doctors in America. Their path is predetermined and difficult. They come here with the degrees with Russian medical institutes when they're already over forty. They have to pass their exams—in English, of course—to get their degree recognized. Then spend a few years in residency (and it's tough to get in!). And they still need time to end up millionaires.

* * *

"And your guts plop down on the sidewalk," writes Dina Rubina about the first days of emigration. In late August and in September of 1996 the Chicago sidewalk is melting from the heat. Our past life falls away into thin air without a trace—as if it never happened. But our new life still hasn't begun...

Everything is the same for everyone. "Depression climbs aboard with a measured pace. The world goes dark." So my friend Olga had said, though now she shares her joy with me: "...right now, it's as if I've been born again. As if the bag over my head has been lifted." (May 1, 2007). For how long though?

* * *

Sasha G. is honest with me: "I sing while I'm driving. Strangely enough, it's always the same two songs. Yuz Aleshkovsky's 'Little Cucumber' and 'Hey, man, raise your collar...' I even sing when I'm driving with my wife. She gets annoyed: the same two songs, year after year." Has anyone considered how songs about the prison camps are a kind of therapy for emigrants? In moments of utter anguish, I often reread Varlam Shalamov's most depressing stories.

* * *

Is emigration a dream? You open your eyes, and there's nothing left. How little is left of Russian émigré literature from the 1920s-30s. We've only heard about the brightest names, many of which were famous even before the Revolution. And how many young talented voices remained unheard. Their works are mentioned as bitter reminders in the letters and diary entries of others. I've discussed this with the literary scholar Oleg Korostelev[31]. He accomplished a miracle: doing the work of an entire institute, he reconstructed the life of the literary emigration in the 20s and 30s. Nevertheless, the gaps in our literary memory are vast, often irreversible. One of the naïve questions that I ask Korostelev: what can we do so that this never happens again? (see our conversation in the journal *Seagull*, 2016, June 10th).

* * *

Fifteen minutes before the Russian bookstore closes, an old lady appears at the door. She wears a white panama hat on her head (a throwback to her pioneer childhood). She carries in her hand a big wallet made of straw, the same one my grandmother used to take to the market. This is clearly not the old lady's first visit to the store: she immediately comes to the shelf with books on esoterica. She's looking for something very intently, hurriedly scanning all the tables of contents.

"Can I help you with anything?" asks the saleswoman.

"No, I got it," the old lady is adamant. But then she looks up at the clock and, realizing that she's come too late and that she'll have to ask for help, says: "I need a book about how to change fate."

Funny? Doubtful. Again, a typical emigrant theme—changing your fate. (2008 April)

* * *

Answering the interview questions from a German magazine *Kreschatyk. Intersection*, which had its anniversary in

2017, I suddenly remember how surprised and happy I was to find 21 Russian-language bookstores when I had just moved to Chicago. Five of them were located very close to my house. Oddly enough each store had its own face. One of them exclusively sold new books, fresh off the plane from Moscow. The owner of another store, a graduate of the Literary Institute, without any considerations of profit, ordered Russian and translated literature that had an experimental vibe. A third drew me in with monographs about art history, albums of artist copies. However, I am certain: the most amazing was a store called the House of the Russian Book. Amid their paintings and engravings, collected works, and many rare editions I could always find something unexpected. And the hospitable owner of this festive kingdom Ilya Rudyak, a writer and director from Odessa, would talk passionately about almost every book, like he was reading poetry. You only had to ask. I would often drop by for Ilya: to talk, to breathe in that special air—no, not of book dust, but the air of Russian culture. By the way, Evgeny Evtushenko, a great bibliophile himself, loved to come here.

...all of these stores have long gone out of business. Their owners, mostly naïve idealists, would go broke. Now there are three kiosks in Chicago that still sell books in Russian: one found its place in a Russian deli, the other two in Russian drugstores.

Of course, American bookstores also constantly go out of business. These multi-story palaces where you often come and spend the whole day. You can not only browse books and magazines to purchase but also sit down and read them. You can also grab a cup of coffee with your friends, even a bite to eat. And again set sail across the sea of books. It's just that there are fewer and fewer seafarers.

Leaving for America, it was painful to bid farewell to my personal library, which I had collected for twenty years with a passion I couldn't quite understand myself. Many shared my feelings. And now it's the Reader that we're biding farewell to. He is going away with frightening speed. And more often it seems that emigrant publications are read only by their own authors.

* * *

An invasion of fortunetellers, clairvoyants, ancestral sorcerers. The Siberian shaman Ayun-batyr cures infertility in individual seances. The contactee Bonifaty changes your fate... my friend MK once paid a visit to a contactee. "He help you?" "So much! And I'm lucky: I bought the privilege of contacting Bonifaty at any time without a line. I can call him, get his advice on any difficult situation in my life."

"And how much did it cost?" MK hesitates, doesn't want to say—moreover, that's not what people do in the West. But then she remembers that we're friends. And spills: "Five thousand."

MK didn't inherit her money. I sincerely admire this stout, aged, but still beautiful woman for her valiant resistance to emigration. She came to America at age 50. No English. With a seriously ill husband and two teenage daughters. One time she explained to me: "One daughter is from a previous marriage, the other from this one; my husband died in a year, I had to do something quick..." Like many others, she chose to clean apartments. She was learning English at the time, picked up driving a car, passed the exam that confirmed her qualifications as a lab chemist (though in a past life, she was a research chemist, the head of a big lab), counted every dollar, paid for her daughters' college, bought a good apartment.

MK is not an idiot. But she is lonely: her daughters have their lives. Then she got diagnosed with cancer. So she had a choice: go into surgery or wait. The contactee—a sweet young man with a decisive gaze—gave the advice MK wanted to hear: wait. After consulting the doctors, MK decides to go for the surgery. "Do you still talk with Bonifaty?" I ask a few months later. "He's hard to get a hold of," MK says without judgment. Maybe she's says so still thinking about some higher power that will intervene in her life.

* * *

On the cover of the Chicago Russian community weekly is a portrait of a priest in church garb. His words in quotes jump out at you: "I beg forgiveness from everyone!" Mikhail Ts., a priest at the Apostle Orthodox church gives an interview. In which he fervently repents for his sins. Back in Kyiv in 1978 he dreamed of becoming a priest, but instead became a KGB agent. M. Ts. chose his own pseudonym — Athos. (This pseudonym was not chosen at random: the future Father was an accomplished fencer). Having parted ways with the KGB and arrived in the US, M. Ts. felt a different calling for himself. He started making international driver's licenses for undocumented Mexican immigrants. But one day "the special forces turned up out of the blue and called me nearly the godfather of the Russian mafia in Chicago... I got out on bail, but with probation." All of this was long ago, twenty years ago. Still his voice is shaking: "...today I beg forgiveness from everyone for my sins and mistakes." But no, there's more. M. Ts. ends by giving gift to his readers: "In Chicago I am the only priest who will, given our "military situation," hear confessions over the phone... completely free of charge, of course." (April 2018)

* * *

Do you anticipate your own death? The answer is obvious. A flood of stories come to mind. But I'll stick to telling just one, my own.

Like everyone, I had heard many times about the robberies in the "disadvantaged" areas of Chicago. The advice of seasoned veterans: never under any circumstance should you argue, run away, resist, or call for help... You should give everything you can, everything they ask for. The best advice: keep some bills in your pocket (what if it's a drug addict in altered state that attacks? He will shoot or beat you up without a second thought).

The other Saturday I'm walking home from the synagogue around 1 pm. It was raining in the morning, but now it's dry and a bit frosty. As I'm walking, I start thinking to myself: "There you go, life has passed me by... No, not like that... The vagueness of my boyhood and youth is gone. Everything ahead is crystal clear. The only thing left to know: what's the end going to be like and when will it come..."

They say when souls descend into this world in order to take on bodily form, the exact date of our departure is already set. So is our mission for coming here. Suddenly, the Almighty gives you a choice: you control the route of your earthly life. But the final date cannot be changed.

Such banal thoughts...

My walk back home takes about fifteen minutes. Suddenly from one of the alleys (near a construction site where they're raising modest two-million-dollar mansions) two boys run out to catch up with me. They are Black, look to be around 18 years old, well-dressed. One of them overtakes me, stretches out his hand: "Good shabbos!"

Then sudden he switches into a menacing tone: "Give us your money... quick... or I'll start shooting."

His hand drops into his pocket, gets out a pistol, then hides it again, pointing the barrel at me through his coat.

Why am I so calm? Maybe because I am remembering my own thoughts from a few minutes ago. Could it be that the Almighty had prepared me for this kind of death?

"I don't have any money." It's true. On the Sabbath, Jews aren't supposed to carry around any cash.

The boys look at one another. The street is still empty.

"I'm going to count to three... one... two..."

He counts to eight. And I'm waiting for the shot. Could this really be? Is this it?

As someone has given me a hint, I take off my new Italian coat:

"This is for you!"

Finally understanding that I really have no money on me and totally ignoring my coat, they turn around and walk away.

* * *

Four days later this still looks quite strange.

It's strange: on the Sabbath in our largely Orthodox Jewish neighborhood there were no pedestrians on the street (the synagogues had just finished their services). It's strange that the boys had appeared here. And that they had disappeared silently.

* * *

Was that a rehearsal of the departure or just a daytime dream?

2018

Rereading Silence

For us there is nothing more important than memory. And nothing less fragile — perhaps only ourselves.

A Hassidic teacher of mine was perspicacious in observing: "Memory is liberation." However, at the end of life, his memory failed him. They say that once, in the middle of a big speech, he stopped all of a sudden. He had forgotten what he was talking about.

It's awkward and painful for me to admit when my memory fails me. Of course, this didn't start happening just now, at life's twilight. It began from my life's very dawning.

* * *

How does this picture from my past appear within me? Believe it or not — it comes as a smile. When I was in second grade, I first encountered an obstacle that would come up time and again. We were assigned to memorize a poem for class. Without much effort the poem would take up residence within me. But then... two-three weeks later it would fly away from me forever. Only individual lines would remain. It was a shame: not only would my efforts be for naught — I could be mistakenly relegated to the ranks of lazybones and dropouts. That's when I realized that I had to make sure to get called on in class to recite my poem. Right away. While I still had it.

Wasn't it that way with all subjects in school? Just about. The only assignments I could do without exerting myself were dictations, book reports, and essays. Well of course here

I could rely on my visual memory—it helped that I had been infected with a passion for reading from the age of seven.

I didn't tell anyone about my *peculiarity*. It was obvious that something was wrong with me, but I didn't get upset. "It is what it is, I guess."

Catastrophe struck—not that anyone noticed—in 7th grade. Chemistry, physics, math... I would get As and Bs on individual assignments. But it was all mechanical. I didn't really get any of it. After 8th grade I switched over to night school. Each subject was broken up into individual credit hours, and each of those I had to pass. That was it for me!

Meanwhile at 14 I was already writing proper articles—some truly big pieces—for the youth paper. I started out writing on "the problems at school," then moved onto film and theater reviews.

University. Journalism major. Again, I was preparing for an exam in a few days. I encountered the same task: passing the exam, and fast. After a week I didn't remember the material too well. After a month—it was almost forgotten. The history of the Soviet press, political economy, the foundations of scientific atheism, history of the Communist Party etc. etc. All of this had happily and completely fallen into the hole of oblivion. However, journalism majors had to study the history of Russian and foreign literatures like the philology students do. And that material *stuck* with me! I came to happy conclusion that my memory gladly accepts what it finds interesting and meaningful. Alas, this law is not absolute. I still can't memorize a *single* poem. Even the ones I love dearly. When I started lecturing myself, I shamefully had to read famous poems out of a book or my notes.

What had happened to me? Only in the latter half of my life I got to "investigating." And then I think some things became clear. I was sent to kindergarten when I was three. That's right: not a daycare, but kindergarten. My mom was working in the local department of education and was able to *arrange* it. One evening when she brought me home, she discovered that her son had stopped talking. In the morning, she interrogated my kindergarten teachers: what had happened to me? As it turned out, while the children were being led out for a walk during the day, I had fallen into a deep hole; a dog had leapt in after me; at first, my disappearance went unnoticed: I was small and had been walking apart from the group... A great fright. I was silent for a whole year. My parents were panicked, turned to professor at the medical institute who worked wonders with hypnosis for help. He refused to treat me: I was too young. Through mutual friends, we eventually talked him into it. He cured me. But perhaps that's why I started getting these holes in my memory?

All my life I try to take account of all possible "holes." When I write articles on literary scholarship or criticism, I check every fact several times. To keep myself accountable, I even draw checkmarks on the margins of the manuscript.

* * *

Do I remember the taste of silence? I think I do. A particular, wordless kind of communication with the world. When speech returns to me, I often ask myself questions: why do we call a chair "chair," why can't an apple be called "plum?"

Then these questions are themselves forgotten. They've wandered off. But poets never forget these questions.

* * *

In January of 1992 I called the Harry Fischel Institute for Talmudic Research to speak with the kabbalist and wiseman rabbi Adin Steinsaltz. I asked him for a meeting: I wanted to ask him questions that, it seemed, I need to have answered to go on living.

"Rabbi Steinsaltz is busy these days. How long are you going to be in Israel?"

"Another month. When can I call you again?"

"Don't worry. We'll find you."

Of course, I thought this was a polite excuse: I myself didn't even know where I was going tomorrow. But sure enough, two weeks later in Haifa when I had returned home to my friends after a night out, I heard: "Rabbi Steinsaltz called. He will see you."

Steinsaltz greeted me with an expected phrase: "I have a gift for you." He explained, "I give you your family as a gift." He handed me a stack of Xeroxed pages from Jewish encyclopedias. They were articles about the Tseytlins—famous rabbis, writers, bankers. Steinsaltz had no doubts: like the majority of Soviet Jews, I knew nothing about my ancestors. Alas, that was indeed the case.

"But couldn't these be just people with the same surname?" I meekly asked.

"Russian Jews only got surnames relatively recently—tracing the genealogy is quite straightforward. I have been researching the surname Tseytlin myself. Isn't true that your father was born in Mogilev or in Shklov?"

...Yes, my dad Lev Grigogrievich Tseytlin (1920–1980) was born in Mogilev. In the 30s our family ended up in Siberia—most likely exiled there, but dad didn't like talking about that. And my mom came from a family of Siberian Jews. A curious paradox linked with the Pale of Settlement: before the revolution, Jews were not allowed in Siberia. There were rare exceptions—including former cantonists, like my mom's grandfather. I remember well my grandpa Abrasha—gray mustache and beard, white linen suit; he was a tailor-dress cutter who worked for nearly ninety years. He would take me, a little boy, to the Omsk synagogue before it burned down completely in a single day.

* * *

I recorded my conversation with Steinsaltz on a tape recorder. However, I was unable to recover the recording. At first, I thought there was something wrong with the tape itself. But then I read a journalist's account of how she interviewed Steinsaltz: "What a shame that only a memory of our conversation remained. The tape recorder only got a record of our silence."

* * *

My mom passed away five years ago. She was ninety, but wanted to keep living and could have lived even longer. She shyly told me stories about people who had easily lived beyond a hundred. And I had happily replied, "And so will you." She didn't have any of the "scary" diseases. According to statistics, perhaps not the most accurate of them, the cause for around 40% deaths in the US was medical malpractice, a doctor's mistake. The mistake that proved fatal for my mom was that she had had a prescription for Vicodin for 20 years. The drug had helped with her arthritis, deadening the pain in her wrists. But as a side-effect she had hallucinations. Mom started to have long conversations with her great-granddaughter's portrait. The great-granddaughter in question was, of course, many kilometers away. She also "saw" Roma dancers on the decorative balcony of her apartment. And sometimes she would swear that there was someone peering into her room through the peephole in the door. I told my mom's doctor all of this many times. She tried to comfort me, "No surprises there. Eighty percent of my patients find themselves in that state. Let me have a guess what your mom is seeing." And she guessed right. But then she would lie to me for some reason: "There's no cure for hallucinations yet."

A few months before her death, mom started confusing me with her late husband, my father.

"Lev," she'd ask me calmly, "What's new with you?"

Lev, who I really had come to resemble, had been dead for thirty-five years.

"It's me, Yevsey, your son."

A sly smile from my mom. She was clearly trying to figure out the truth. But with no success. The next day she would ask, "So who was the one who came here—my son or my husband?"

Then her mind would clear. But sometimes at the hospital, when the doctors would try to make sure that she was with it, she couldn't remember her own name. Sometimes she'd say the wrong name, one that more clearly spoke to her inner state at that moment. Mom was born in 1926, her name was Ninel. I didn't figure out until later that this was Lenin backwards. She herself, I should add, never complained about her parent's choice of name for her.

Mom was a strong personality. How could I compete with her! When she was a student at the technical institute, she broke the head of an anti-Semitic upperclassmen. She refused to ask for forgiveness and was kicked out of the institute. The war was going on; in order to receive rations, a young girl at the time, she started working at the factory. Once she received a telegram: her brother would be passing by Omsk on the way to the front lines. The head of the union (himself Jewish, by the way) refused her request to go to the train station to meet him. She threw the details she was working on in his face. She didn't get sued, but was sent to work on the press line. There, mom lost half of her index finger on her right hand.

To this day I blame myself for fighting with her. The reason was banal: in her 90s, mom was sure that nothing bad could happen to her. There was no way she could catch a cold. It was hard to get her to put on a scarf, never mind a winter coat. Only one argument could convince her: "Tomorrow you're going to catch pneumonia, and I'm the one who's going to have to take care of you."

Of course, I was happy to take care of her. The last month of her my mom was in a coma. But whenever I would come visit her in the hospital, I would always freeze up in anticipation of the coming joy: I'm about to see my mom.

* * *

At a concert of the violinist Igor Bezrodny when I first laid eyes on my future wife, I instantly got the feeling: this is a kindred spirit. Regina was very beautiful, but I didn't notice that at the time for some reason. On the contrary, for many years I was annoyed that others would notice that about her. She was a student: naturally, a future philologist. But before that she had finished nursing school and was working as a nurse-practitioner with a surgeon in a hospital. We met at my favorite train station. She would arrive at the station, tired after being on call all night. We drank coffee with cognac. And we sat there in silence, scared to predict the future.

* * *

Two days after our wedding we moved to Kyrgyzstan to teach Russian in a village school. Why Kyrgyzstan? In the hall of arrivals there stood a strange contraption: an automated information desk. Once, after deciding to get married, we were standing by it and started poking each of the buttons. The names of two cities endlessly far away from Omsk—Frunze and Tallinn—flashed before us. The choice was predetermined: the East had always fascinated me. And Regina was already onboard with my choice.

* * *

Our aul was logically divided—from our perspective!—into two halves. One half contained the school and electricity. In the other half stood the house we were given. There was no electricity there, but we did have a view of the mountains from our window.

We would take long hikes in the mountains in winter and fall—until the cold settled in. It seemed that the mountains had seen a great deal, but kept their memories and wisdom to themselves in silence.

There weren't that many children at the local school. They looked at Regina and me as if we were exotic birds that had accidently flown into their world. Of course, in a sense they were right. They spoke Russian poorly and could barely write it. They would mix up the meanings of words. Girls would huddle close to Regina, inhaling the unfamiliar scent of her dress.

Our landlord was a 40-year-old Kyrgyz man, who was drunk all the time. His name was Nurbek. Sometimes we were happy to see him, other times he frightened us. He shaved his head till it shone: it looked as if his face started at the nape of his neck. He had been well beloved in the aul for a long time. The reason for this love were his two professions. First, he was a good veterinarian. Second, he performed the circumcisions for the local Kyrgyz boys. Not on the eighth day of the boy's life, like Jews do it, but when the boys were three, five or seven. I asked Nurbek about the technical side of this sacred Muslim practice.

"Nothing interesting there," he lazily swatted away my question. I also tried to figure out why this respectable citizen of the aul regularly beats his wife within an inch of her life.

She was about 10 years younger than her husband and also taught chemistry at our school. However, it seemed that she had a schedule that was more important to her than the list of her classes. Now and then Gulzhan would ride off on a motorcycle or just walk on foot into the mountains—it seemed she'd be off with the first guy that caught her eye. Moreover, she wasn't shy at all around her mother-in-law—a constantly yelling old women that took care of her five kids. That old woman, by the way, wasn't shy around my wife and me.

When Nurbek would tie her hands with rope and beat her, Gulzhan was silent. Maybe she didn't want to frighten her kids, whom her mother-in-law took to the farthest room of the house. Gulzhan always pursed her lips and glared at her husband.

The simplest and most inaccurate explanation for all this would be to assume a painful and unsurmountable passion on her part. This was a woman raised in a traditional Muslim community after all. I thought that there was something else that was bothering her. Nobody kept other people's secrets in the aul. Or maybe they felt no need to hide anything from us as "fleeting passersby." A month later we heard Gulzhan's bitter and sympathetic story. She was taking revenge on her husband. She was only fifteen when he had raped her, drunk as always, taking her away to those same ancient mountains.

* * *

Sometimes we would hear an echo from the outside world that now seemed so far away. In that world everything was the same as it was here: people lived, dreamed, suffered, and died; someone silently yet firmly determined the paths of their fates.

The mailman would come in on horseback. Once he brought me a letter from Varya, a teacher from the Siberian town of T. (Varya had sent her letter to the Omsk address, and mom had put it in another envelope and sent it to Kyrgyzstan). I instantly remembered that town with its little port and wooden sidewalks; it's an ideal town to spent your retirement in—quiet, lots of greenery, just beyond the outskirts there's a grove where below the birch trees bloom beautiful lungworts—these gentle dark blue flowers. I was there on a business trip a year ago. Only for a few days. I judged an essay contest for the seniors at the local high school on the topic "My dreams at the doorstep of a bright future" and published the winners in their youth paper. Varya and her friend Zina, who taught the senior's literature classes, treated me to tea with candies and pies, showed me around the local sites to see, and finally saw me off onto my ship. As a parting gift they gave me a collection of Pasternak's poems, published in the *Poet's Library* minor series.

Now Varya was writing to tell me she wasn't doing well: in late fall her father died. He was buried in the new graveyard beyond the city limits. The ground there was unsuitable for a grave, all rocks, the gravediggers were cursing as they worked—and Varya cried the whole time.

Varya also informed me that seven of the seniors, who shared "their dreams" with me, had ended up in prison: "three of them ended up there for larceny, four of them—for hooliganism." Back at school everything's same, except the old principal Kapustin ("You met him, right?") retired and is working on an article about Pushkin's realism in "The Captain's Daughter." The church, closed in 1930, got turned into a children's sports academy. The canteen now gets all the best candies—"Squirrel" and "Bear in the North," not only "Tatiana in the South"—that cheap and sticky caramel. In the evenings she and Zina drink tea in Zina's grandmother's garden, come down to the river to sit and listen to the heavy waves of the Irtysh River for a while.

After I finished the letter, I turned off the kerosene lamp, pulled Regina's comforter over her, and walked over to the window. I got to thinking about these people whom, in all likelihood, I would never see again. Varya, Zina, and I had become colleagues unexpectedly. Varya was endlessly lonely— otherwise she probably wouldn't have written such a confessional letter to me, a person, in all honesty, she barely knew. It was good to hear about the old man Kapustin, though. All his life he had worked as a math teacher, had survived two heart surgeries, would probably die soon, but was still thinking the problems of realism in Pushkin novella, not at all concerned by the fact that nobody cared about his research.

* * *

A little tome of Isaac Babel. And a small, clearly castrated collection of notes "through the eyes of his contemporaries." I found both books at the local library and never want to return them. Time and again—either clearly or faintly—Babel reminds me of the famous words from Ecclesiastes: "Ashes to ashes, dust to dust..." Times and again Babel interrogates ancient truths. The most obvious of them. He'll tell one of his acquaintances—T. Stakh—that he witnessed "the cremation of Eduard Bagristky[32]. They let him go down there, where they don't let anybody go, where he could observe the whole process through a special peephole. He told how the body was lifted in the flames, how he forced himself to see this horrifying spectacle."

* * *

...And in Kyrgyzstan near the mountains wrinkled by age, I returned to the same question: what does one live for? The question was not an abstract one. Near our home in a small yurt lived an old man, who lost his wits—so people said—forty years ago. That was during collectivization. The old man was deemed a kulak and had his property expropriated—and with it his mind. Three of his wives were sent to Siberia. The man stayed there in his frail little yurt, poorly insulated from the wind in winter. From spring to late fall he would sit on a dirty felt rug, catching the sun on his face. The first time I came down to the aqueduct, the old man kindly asked me for a cigarette. I didn't smoke, but soon started buying unfiltered "White Sea Canal" cigarettes for my new friend. After she finished her classes for day, my wife would cook dinner on the kerosene stove, a gift from the school principal Dzhipara Osmanoliyevna. I would start coming down to the aqueduct quite frequently. Though we never discussed this, I would meet up with Sabir—that was the old man's name. We would sit on the shore on huge boulders and watch the lively water playing with rocks. I soon discovered that my new friend was completely normal. It seemed that his neighbors had never doubted this. But he didn't come out into the village because, as I found out, the old man had enemies in the aul. However, it wasn't like anybody could denounce him—the one-man show of "Crazy Old Man" had been running for many years and was directed by a professional. Even now Sabir, many decades later, seemed to be the most educated person in the area. He calmly told me that he had graduated from a prep school. He still faintly remembered the couple languages he had studied and had excellent Russian. Of course, Sabir had studied all the symptoms of his fake illness and could trick doctors with ease.

The aul dwellers treated me and my wife hospitably. They would often have us over. But soon we also found our small community of "Russians": this community consisted of two Jews (my wife and me), the German school secretary, and a Ukrainian nurse-practitioner. One time the young PE teacher invited us over to his house. He was still single and lived with his parents. Of course, there was a motive behind the invitation: my first guess was that the young man had taken a liking to one of the "Russian" young women. When we came over, however, he didn't seem to spend much time with them. I did end up having a long conversation with the teacher's grandfather. He had noticed that I spent a lot of time with crazy old Sabir. It turned out that my old man was once fabulously wealthy: he owed many flocks of sheep. Apparently, he had seduced many beautiful women in the aul, though he later organized their weddings. Any villager that dared oppose him was harshly punished. How? "He'd stuff them in a leather bag and throw them in to the aqueduct. Often they would be badly hurt and bruised."

The next day I didn't ask Sabir about any of this. I just asked him how he managed to fulfil his duties as a man while courting so many women. The old man didn't realize I was joking. He told me that you needed to learn to make pigeon soup. In fact, you could even roast the birds. I carefully wrote the recipe down, but ended up losing it since I didn't really need it.

What did Sabir teach me? Nothing. It was good sit next to him in silence. Psychologists believe that silence mysteriously communicates all the essential information about a person. I would sit next to Sabir and slowly read his life, the one he had left and the one he had taken on. Maybe that was the content of his lesson. Nothing new. The only things that are eternal are the mountains, the sky, and the frozen water in the aqueduct.

In the winter the former rich man would go into hibernation. The other villagers would be worried, peering into his home: is he alive? They would leave behind flatbread and bottles of ayran—a sour milk drink.

Towards the New Year we discovered that Regina was pregnant. After sending her off to her parents, I took up teaching the Russian classes at the school. Sabir and I didn't see each that often anymore. It seemed to me that he, like myself, was getting bored without our meetings. In the summer after grading the final exams I left the aul, never to return again.

Before catching the bus to the regional capital, I came up to the familiar yurt. It was empty. I didn't have time to go looking for Sabir. I bid farewell to him silently—I placed two packets of unfiltered cigarettes on his faded cotton blanket.

* * *

"Don't you think that your granddaughter knows something you don't?" Alina L. once asked me. I want to take out the question make. Well, of course. "A fresh soul, untroubled by anything material. That's where it comes from." Liba B. added.

I shuddered when, on the second day after she was born, I felt my granddaughter's bright and severe gaze on me. I remembered a story from the Haggadah, an immortal collection of Jewish wisdom. It is believed that babies when they are in their mothers' wombs already know the entirety of the Torah. But when a baby emerges into the world, an angel smacks them on the lips: the sacred knowledge must be forgotten for now.

I remember discovering my daughter's gaze on me, just as bright and severe. She was five. And she was honestly and successfully smashing all the toys she could get her hands on. At one point I couldn't take it anymore and I smacked her on her bottom a few times. Suddenly I heard: "What are you doing? You can't do that! You can't hit a child!" And I saw my daughter staring at me, her gaze not guaranteeing any forgiveness.

* * *

In 2003–4, the diary of Eugène Ionesco was always on my mind—more accurately, selections from his diaries throughout his life (Moscow, 1992). I put bookmarks on the pages I wanted to return to. One such passage, for example: "Death makes reality into something paltry, something unreal. To me, death seems to be the only truth, the only thing that is final. It is a wall that you can't look behind."

Once when I was in Paris, I easily found Ionesco at the Montparnasse Cemetery. He had died sixteen years ago (1994). Now his wife is buried beside him. The diaries revealed that he had been so concerned about her fate (without him).

When I got back home, I returned to his unconditionally honest book. And I hear old age dragging its feet across the floor. Ionesco describes how he and his wife had stayed in an old castle that then belonged to a dramaturgy society. "With great discomfort and shame, the author shared his "completely personal anxiety": "the wonderful castle from the 18th century, where we are staying, is poorly equipped in terms of sanitation facilities. In the small corner of our room (the most beautiful in all the castle) there is a shower, a toilet, a bidet even... but this "small corner" is meant to accommodate multiple people; at the moment we are 18 people... our floor has only two bathrooms..." It seems that that was what concerned him the most at the time. But no: "How surprising and frightening it is to entirely forget our own names! [...] My anxiety emerges from a fear of empty spaces, a fear of gaping holes: the holes of non-existence. Without my wife's help it's hard for me to remember the name of that English actor who played Bérenger in the London production of *Rhinoceros* (now I remember that that was Laurence Olivier)... I can't remember the name of that Russian, that poet, who won the Nobel Prize, but they wouldn't let him leave the country to receive it... but ahh, I've got it—it was Boris (?) Pasternak."

The creator of the "theater of the absurd" spoke quietly, almost in a whisper.

Someone in the Mirror

It's best when it's quick — and unintentional — the glance at the mirror.

Deep wrinkles on the brow.

The beard I forget to trip. (Before it had a little gray; now it's dotted by patches of black).

A traditional yarmulka.

Why don't I recognize myself in the mirror?

This is a typical collision between your youthful, or better yet eternal, soul and your shrinking, fairly worn-out mortal coil.

Despite the mirror we feel young for a long time. The realization that you're not comes suddenly. When people your age start passing away, one by one.

* * *

The writer AL, an old friend of mine from Siberia, found me on the internet. He wrote to me about his career with measured pride: he published around ten books, became a respected man of letters... He still lived on the street where we wandered together half a century ago. Of course, I asked Aleksandr about our mutual friends, those whom we worked with at the newspaper, our fellow Writers' Union members. He gave the same answer time and again: dead. Sometimes there were particular details about their respective deaths. For example, V, the former youth newspaper editor, always gentle and smiling, liked to turn his bathroom into a sauna. One day, he couldn't get out. "It seems he was boiled alive," wrote Aleksandr.

"Man is like grass; his days are wildflowers—they bloom and die. The wind passes over—and he is no more, his place no longer recognizes him," as the Psalms tell us.

* * *

Any writer who has enough wise patience to soberly examine their own works and the works of those who have walked the literary path before them sooner or later will ask themselves: so why am I dragging my proverbial quill across the page? Since Lermontov and Tolstoy, Goncharov and Chekhov, Bunin and Nabokov have all done it before me? Thinking I'm special is naïve. I'm doing this just because of the tireless graphomaniac sitting inside me. And for some, writing is difficult, at time torturous.

Every person's soul descends into this world on some mission. For some, that mission is writing.

* * *

From a very young age I was sure that there was a mystery I needed to solve.

At first, I sought answers in books. By twelve, I had hurriedly worked my way through a library of Russian and Western classics.

At fifteen, I started working as a professional journalist.

At nineteen, I got married and moved to a Kyrgyz aul to teach Russian and, more importantly, to spend time with the village elders, the Aqsaqals.

The latter goal defined my life for many years. Those years ears consisted of work trips and meetings. Those years now flash before me as in a kaleidoscope: the faces of Siberian shamans, secret yoga instructors, the vanishing populations of Russia's native northern peoples, pathology labs, the eyes of blind prophets, monasteries, yeshivas, archival reading rooms...

All of my books began with a mystery, though they are all about artists. My very first book, the work of a young man, is about learning to find inspiration in order to become a writer. My protagonists were Vsevolod Ivanov, one of the brightest and most enigmatic representatives of the Russian literary avant-garde of the 1920s, and pastor Kristijonas Donelaitis[33], the founder of modern Lithuanian literature... I was mostly drawn to talents that had not yet been able to fully realize themselves, when the artists had only begun to recognize their mission in life, stars that flashed across the literary horizon—before being snuffed out.

* * *

I'm reading an interview with the poet Tomas Venclova[34]. He was recounting his first meetings with Anna Akhmatova[35] and what she thought about younger poets. Akhmatova was always generous with her praise, said that it was impolite to criticize... But the young poets around her knew well that if she actually like your poems, she'd say: "You have a secret."

* * *

There's something peculiar about me. As a young writer, why would I pick the most "boring" genres to work in: literary criticism and scholarship?

There was no inspiration sent from on high. I had justice on my mind.

"...Manuscripts don't burn, but human destinies do. Here's a bitter fate, still unwritten, from the annals of our literary history." That's how I began my book *Writer in the Provinces* (Moscow, 1990). In 70s and 80s, I had written many articles and reviews of talent writers from the Soviet provinces and "peripheries" that went unnoticed in literary criticism from "the capitals." I had publications in many journals and collections as well as a series of seven monographs... Alas, all of this did little to change my protagonists' fates.

* * *

Is it an irony of fate or just fate itself that I have spent half a century reading other writers' manuscripts?

What surprises me the most in this constant flow of writing? No, it's not the various spelling mistakes. It's the banality of the thoughts I read. Everything's made up of literary cliches that successfully travel not only across decades, but across centuries.

* * *

What makes an author reach for a cliché? It's easy to write it off as laziness or to call them a graphomaniac. I think there's a different reason: a lack of attention. After all, attention is the foundation of a writer's talent.

* * *

In the Soviet Union, there was a long-standing discourse about the necessity for a writer to "study real life." They were sent with this expressed mission to the Arctic Circle, to the virgin lands, at least to the local factory. At same time, writers must remain attentive to themselves first and foremost. The process of self-discovery is one of the of the most important "studies of real life" for a writer to undertake. That's why there is no exaggeration in Gustave Flaubert's famous pronouncement, "I am Madame Bovary."

* * *

Writers have to be interested in themselves. Does that sound strange? Call it egocentricism and narcissism, call it whatever you want. But without this avid interest in themselves, an author can never hope to unlock the mysteries of the human soul.

* * *

Ignorance is undoubtedly one of the main qualities of today's "young writer." At least in the émigré community, where I've been living thirty years. These young writers know maybe five or six names: Akhmatova, Mandelstam, Tsvetaeva, Pasternak, Brodsky, Dovlatov... And they are so sure of their "uniqueness." God forbid they lose it under the weight of extra reading!

* * *

Why must a writer know both their literary ancestors and contemporaries? There are a couple answers, and they're all correct. To avoid repeating the past. To feel connected to a living literary tradition. To load up with energy for the endless pursuit of their aesthetic goals.

* * *

In the late 80s, when the Soviet empire was breathing its last, I began recording Soviet Jews' oral histories. I didn't come to decision right away—funny enough, it came to me in a dream. Nearly every night I would dream of an old Jewish man with big, sad eyes. He was always silent, and, paradoxically, seemed to be asking me for something. After I woke up, I tried to think—what was his request? Finally, it dawned on me: millions of people (several generations), I thought, would disappear into oblivion without the opportunity to tell their truth about the time, when the very word "Jew" was nearly unpronounceable in the languages of the USSR.

After many months I realized how sharply I had changed my life—nearly snapped it in two. I had gone from being a successful literary scholar and critic, an associate professor to running around as oral historian, chasing after people's fates.

...The exodus from the land of the communist pharaohs was becoming massive. I heard stories—at once unbelieve, but somehow ordinary at the same time—from activists working with recently created Jewish organizations, from former prisoners of the ghettos and concentration camps. I listened to involuntary confessions in lines to the consulate. I met with authors working in Yiddish, their widows and children: more often than not, these were people whose souls were forever marred by fear.

In the early 90s, my wife and I moved to Lithuania, a country that at the time was trying to secede from the Soviet Union. Though undeniably brave, the attempt was seen by many as suicidal. My friends and family all thought that our decision to move was unexpected, even dangerous. However, now I see that it was one of the best decisions I ever made. First of all, I had often kept the small republic's struggle for independence in my heart. My book about Kristijonas Done-laitis had been published both in Russian and in Lithuanian, and the pastor was considered the founder of modern Lithu-anian literature, but also the spiritual grandfather of Sąjūdis, the Lithuanian independence party. Second of all, I decided that Lithuania was where it made the most sense to continue my project recording Jewish oral histories—Lithuanian Jews had by and large avoided the winds of assimilation.

...The country was rushing to throw off the ice-cold armor of Soviet dogma. But it took a while for people to defrost. It often felt as if my interview subjects were looking around in their minds "Where am I?" They all seemed to have the same question on their minds: "What happened to our souls after all these decades?" They often treated my tape recorder as a chance for confession, a chance to purify themselves and get back to their essence. I developed a special system for con-ducting interests. My psychologist friends later told me in re-minded them of Freud's method.

My notebooks filled up with the "dreams of Soviet Jews." I hope that solving them would let me understand my sub-jects' silences.

* * *

What was the most difficult part of writing this book for me?

What will this book open up in your own fate, what will it clarify in your life? Those are the questions that are the hard-est for me to answer. There is, however, nothing peculiar in asking yourself these questions. After all, every author writes for themselves, first and foremost.

* * *

It's been nearly a quarter of a century since my book *Long Conversations in Anticipation of a Joyous Death* (1996) was published by the Jewish Museum of Lithuania. It's had a life of its own. Critics have written about it; it's been translated into Lithuanian, German, Ukrainian, Spanish, and English. But now, correcting a manuscript for a Russian reprint, I am shocked to observe that many details, entire passages of text have been completed wiped from my memory.

I do, however, remember how I wrote the book.

It was an unusual experiment. I conducted it for five years together with my protagonist Jokubas Josade[36] (in my journal that served as the basis of my book, I referred to him as y).

I was recording a severely ill y's confession at death's threshold. Having travelled a path typical for an intellectual of his generation (a life made up of illusions, betrayals, and ever-present fear), y longed for confession. I, on the other hand, was trying to plunge deep into another's consciousness, past the thick layers of psychological cliches. I was not just curious to hear about the external, admittedly tragic, entanglements of the "wolf-hound age," as Mandelstam called it, and this man's fragile fate. We talked about the motifs of endless compromises in his life, of his constant self-denigration of his talents. y actively chose to hide his gifts in order to survive. After the war, when the Soviet anti-Semitic campaigns began in earnest, Jankel Josade changes his name and working language. Before he had been a Yiddish prose writer; now, he decided to become—with great difficulty—a Lithuanian critic and dramaturg.

...Throughout the years, I often return to the same questions. I do, at times, receive differing answers. A paradox of human consciousness.

During these five years, the concept of a "joyous death" took on different meanings in our conversations. Sometimes it signaled returning (at least, at the end of one's life) to yourself, to your immortal soul, a soul you had forgotten about and which reminded you of itself. At the very edge of his life on earth, j confesses: "My dear, I don't need anything. Not a single thing... You know, the absence of pain is itself happiness. Precisely so: the absence of pain. This *absence* intoxicates you, and then you feel drowsy. You are swimming somewhere—farther and farther away. What can be better than that? Farther and farther away... That is all.

* * *

From the author's introduction:
"...The thoughts, the consciousness of a person, approaching death. That is the object of my account. That is what dictates my intonation, defines my plot..."

* * *

Why are people frightened by the very word 'death'?
"I am not ready to read your book," the New York-based writer B. N. tells me.

A famous Russian press is ready to publish *Long Conversations in Anticipation of a Joyous Death*, but makes an ultimatum: "You absolutely must change the title. It could scare off many readers." I couldn't accept this condition. My main goal was to reconstruct a person's consciousness in light of death.

I'll add that in Judaism the death of the physical body is merely a pitstop of our immortal soul's path to new life.

* * *

The book was also experimental in the sense that it could be read in multiple ways. The author tries to avoid any "trends," distances himself from his subject, but at the same time becomes his protagonist's "mirror."

"Write this book yourself," the author addresses the reader directly. He insists that the reader should build their own narrative, dedicated to y, from the block-like chapters.

* * *

In November 2016 I received a letter from the Russian-French writer Nikolai Konstantinovich Bokov: "...now and then, I read your work and find myself greatly resonating with it. Could I send you *Fragmentarium*, my most recent book?"

Our friendship was short-lived: on December 2, 2019, Bokov passed away in the Tenon Hosptial in Paris.

"*Fragmentarium*," its author warned me, "is like a planetarium: it's like a constellation of ideas and feelings floating in the cosmos of human life. They disappear and then re-appear as meteorites. Some of the memories I share still burn and bleed, others have long hardened into unhabitable moons. Every person is a cosmos... Every person is a collector of the fragments of their future, merely gluing them together."

Reading this incredible book, I finally understood the reasoning behind Nikolai Bokov's choices in life, which always surprised his contemporaries, falling into a strange narrative for his life.

There's no doubt that Bokov was a talented student of the great Silver Age writer Vasily Rozanov[37]. His long admiration of the classical essayist can be felt throughout all of Bokov's texts. The author formulated one of the main lessons he learned from Rozanov in an interview with Maria Shaburina (2010): "While I was, so to speak, investigating life, I thought that 'living' is not as important as reading books, on the condition that I treat my life as a book that Somebody is writing through me: call that Somebody God, Fate, what have you... I read it by myself, and it will tell me everything about my relationship with the material world and with the ideal world, the world beyond... A harmony lurks behind all horrors and deformities. And this harmony is sweet, for it is paradise and eternity itself."

In these words, I hear the author attempting to sooth himself. What harmony is there to speak of? In the Soviet Union, Bokov was a dissident, a creator and distributor of samizdat from his teenage years. He faced many interrogations by the KGB, was kicked out of his PhD program. Eventually, the System even kicked him out of the country. This was a happy conclusion, in a sense—no time in jail or the camps or in exile. In 1975, more than forty years ago, Bobok reached the West.

Of course, Bokov as a writer is very close to me in his own way. First and foremost, he was relentless in continuing his experimentation. Not only in literature—in his life as well. His entire life was one big experiment. From a young age he started asking himself the questions that later he would direct to his characters: what is a human being? What are we capable of in freedom and in un-freedom? Normally, it's philosopher and teenagers that concern themselves with these questions. Nikolai Bokov remained a teenager at heart and was trained as a philosopher at Moscow State.

In search of an answer to these questions, Bokov kept on changing the genre and style of his books—kept on changing his life. In Paris he lived as a homeless person, as a clochard, sleeping and begging on the streets, testing himself. He spent some time living in a cave, roamed between monasteries, moved from country to country, observing different lifestyles and learning local languages. Throughout his travels, he rarely carried a passport or enough money for tickets. Then he returned to literature and told the world about his search through his books.

What answer did he find at the end of the road? I ask myself the same question, but always find that in life and in literature, the question is far more necessary than the answer.

The Zone of Answers is the name of one of Nikolai Bokov's most important books. He wrote upon returning to the world of "acceptable" society.

Was the author's fate a success? In emigration, every writer inevitably loses their audience of readers without finding a new one. Thankfully, Bokov wasn't too affected by this tendency. He was published in Russian émigré journals, a two-volume set of his works was published in Russia, albeit in Nizhy Novgorod, not in the capitals, with a modest print run—not that it matters. In addition, Bokov had long been writing and getting published in French, even winning French prizes.

The years we were friends, he was not old yet. But his fast-approaching old age is a constant motif in his last letters. Nikolai wanted to make old age a subject for an artistic investigation. And, in doing so, perhaps defeat it? "It's interesting to ask: if you write a book about aging and old age, will anyone read it? Those haven't gotten there yet will say, 'Oh, that doesn't interest me'... those who are already there—'I already know it firsthand, thank you very much.'"

He thought that his old age was approaching. But really it was death knocking at his door.

* * *

It takes seven years for every cell in our bodies to be renewed. And we begin repeating the words that our forefather Abraham heard from the Creator even more often: "Leave your country and go to the land I will show you!" So it goes. Though we can't always see the logic behind that which we timidly call Fate.

Is it a coincidence that it was seven years ago that I moved to Chicago? The external reason for this second emigration was evident: my wife's aging parents were living in Chicago. They needed to be with their daughter, and my wife was afraid that she would never see them again. But is it a coincidence that it was here, in the US, that saw once again "the lonely ones among pedestrians" and discovered the "sequels" to their stories?

* * *

Lonely is the one who makes a choice.

Lonely is the one contemplating their path.

Lonely is the writer, searching for a single word, entirely their own.

Lonely is the one who prays.

Everyone who places their fate in the hands of the Almighty is lonely. And only He is able to help.

* * *

Multiple articles in Russophone publications in Israel eloquently argue that after circumcision male potency does not diminish. These pieces are written in the style of legal defenses. That's why an attentive reader starts to get suspicious— where there's smoke there's fire. I can personally confirm that these suspicions are unfounded. But what's the big deal with circumcision anyway? The thing is, this ritual, the brit milah or bris, is the sign of a Jew's covenant with the Almighty.

In January 1992 I had my circumcision in Israel. It was a cold and gloomy morning. The ceremony was performed in a hotel room in Jerusalem. I was forty-four.

During the circumcision, a Jewish man receives a name. Children have their names chosen by their parents; adults chose their own names. I had no doubts about my choice: Yehoshua. In prerevolutionary Russia, the name Yehoshua was often changed to Yevsey.

In the Torah, when our prophet and teacher Moses was at death's threshold, the Almighty gave one of his disciples Yehoshua, or Joshua, the task of leading the Jewish people to Israel.

* * *

I interviewed many people for my oral history project. I asked many awkward questions, trying to get to the deepest secrets of human life. One time my friend Professor Irena Veisaitė (as a child she survived the Kaunas ghetto before going on to win many international awards) gave me some advice: "You absolutely must interview yourself."

* * *

Unexpectedly, interviewing myself turned out to be difficult. After prepping my questions, I began trying to answer them. But nearly every single time... I would fall asleep. Was my consciousness pushing away self-analysis? I told this to my friend Grigory Yablonsky, a famous chemist. We met in 1968 in Novosibirsk Academic Village. Back then Yablonsky was one of the organizers of a singer-songwriter festival. Now in the US he is a professor at multiple universities, the founder of many original concepts and the author of a few no less original short stories, all built around paradoxical thinking. He was not surprised when I told him about my troubles: "About fifty years ago, back in the later 60s, I was struck by the question—why can't we tickle ourselves? I still can't figure out the answer."

* * *

Will these notes take the place of my failed attempt at an interview?

* * *

One of my goals, to maintain the integrity of my experiment, was to accurately describe my sex life. Its awkward early days, mistakes made by young people burdened by shyness. No, I wasn't brave enough to do it. I wrote down two pages — and immediately crossed them out. What am I shy about? My wife reading it? I hoped I would be able to explain how these pages were a necessary inclusion in my notes. Was I shy in front of potential readers, some of whom could be friends and acquaintances? I freely admit that I don't care what anyone thinks of me anymore. But I would feel uncomfortable if my daughter read these pages. Parents are supposed to remain sinless for their children.

* * *

And once again I recalled Rebbe Rashab's wise words: people consist of three layers. There's the "inner person," the "middle person," and the "outer person." No matter what we experience, no matter how life may break us down, only the other two layers can be damaged. The "inner person" will forever remain untouched.

I'm trying to reach through to that "inner person."

* * *

We are locked into an eternal battle against entropy, the dark force that destroys all our traces.

Here's an interesting suggestion that I received as the editor of the monthly literary and cultural journal *Shalom*: there needs to be an online encyclopedia of articles about the most ordinary people. "The poetry of an ordinary fate is the key to understanding the nature of time."

* * *

"I" or "he"? Always an important choice to make in writing a diary entry. "I" indicates your total dissolution in the material. "He" adds some distance, some defamiliarization.

Now and then, I go with the pronoun "he" in order to look at myself from the outside.

* * *

I came to this realization during a yoga session. I won't go into details. Those who have had a similar experience will understand me immediately.

To look at yourself as at an *other*. You become distanced from yourself. You stop pitying yourself.

* * *

Tamara Vladimirovna Ivanova (Isaac Babel's ex-wife, the widow of Vsevolod Ivanov), one of my most wise and important teachers, told me about this when I was young in early 70s: "Most people never see themselves from the outside. That's the source of all their troubles."

* * *

For many writers, the trouble is an inability to create the necessary distance between themselves and their characters.

* * *

I have written three books about Vsevolod Ivanov. My very first one was called *Conversations on the Road. Literary mentor, critic, editor.* (Novosibirsk, 1977).

* * *

"The unexpected Vsevolod Ivanov!" his contemporaries had many occasions to exclaim. All his life this "oppositional canonized writer" of Soviet literature withdrew not only from the dogmas of socialist realism, but from his earlier work as well. "And so, he died an important writer that we haven't read," as Shklovsky aptly wrote in his memoirs. There's a lot of truth in that. Ivanov left behind an entire collection of unpublished, brilliant, and experimental novels.

"The unexpected Vsevolod Ivanov!" I repeated this phrase as well. It turned out that one Moscow archive contained around three hundred reviews written by the author about the works of young writers. Indeed, Ivanov was an observant and wise literary mentor to many. He taught young writers much, most importantly the importance of artistic searching and eternal doubt, the driving force of creativity.

In my book I tried to reconstruct "the Ivanov school, understand its foundations," and, naturally, define the main stages of the writer's development.

* * *

I read somewhere that for every hundred thousand people, there are two that are completely identical to one another. Perhaps these doubles are our own rare mirrors?

In 1984 he met his own "clone" in Zheleznovodsk in a sanatorium by a hot spring bath. Once, when he was drying his body off with a towel, he looked over and saw: the curtain to the bath next door was drawn open. And there he lay... his double. The man's eyes were closed. He got a good look at him. Same face, same body. Even the same birthmark on his chest. The same appendage shamelessly rising above the water.

Twenty years later in Chicago... he looks at the author photo in the local newspaper. Again, he recognizes an aged version of himself. He calls the double's number, hears a different voice over the phone, invites him to meet up. The voice he hears is unconditionally firm: "Like there aren't so many identical people all over the world." The short argument convinces him: meeting your double is truly unnecessary.

* * *

Does an interest in politics interfere with a poet's work? The question may seem speculative, until you take a concrete example.

In 1987–89 I was taking advanced writing seminars in Moscow. A standout among the students was the Chechen poet Z. Vysoky, a temperamental person who would often talk about the history and struggles of his people with great pain. He gave me a literal translation of his own poems to read, and the poems were just like him: bright and loud. Z.'s family often came to visit him. His eldest, a boy about ten years old, overflowing with energy, was always a source of anxiety for me. Impossible to calm down, he would ride the elevator of our dormitory up and down for hours on end and run around the streets of Moscow. Returning to classes after summer break, I learned that Z's son got hit by a car and died.

It seemed that Z himself was filled to brim with the same energy. The history of independent Chechnya is woven from the ambiguous biographies of its leaders. I often recall the enthusiasm with which Z read his poems out loud in the original.

* * *

Perhaps the most important thing for an author is to find the right genre. The genre has to "rhyme" with the author's temperament, the temperament of their voice, with their unique perspective on life.

* * *

Publishers, worrying about book sales, push writers to the genre of the novel, beloved by mass audiences since time immemorial. And there's a chance for a tragic collision: the talents of many writers don't resonate with the novel as a form. They are better suited for the novella, the short story, or the play. Indeed, the novel itself is often naively seen in a very limited perspective: as if, first and foremost, the novel requires detailed descriptions of life, a jauntily wound-up plot, truths told fearlessly, which usually entails amassing of "life's horrors."

Meanwhile there aren't actually that many real novels being written anymore. Each of them is a complex and distinct architectural construction. The author's own personal philosophy and worldview lies at the foundation of them all.

* * *

In the Soviet Union, the art of writing was taught in a few specialized institutions (e.g. the Literary Institute, the screenplay-writing program of the Gerasimov Institute of Cinematography). In the US, hundreds of colleges and universities have their own "creative writing" program. Does this make people happier and more harmonious?

* * *

There are so many literary awards and prizes. I'm afraid that the reader can't even keep track of all of the Booker and Nobel laureates, not to mention the prizewinners for journals, newspapers, regions, and clubs.

Are prizes being devalued, which is a situation unlikely to further the development of contemporary literature? That was a rhetorical question. The one plus side is that some awards—far too few—come with cash prizes and allow a writer to make a living.

* * *

Literature is moving online. Dina Rubina recalls her friend's longstanding advice: "If you don't exist on the internet, you don't exist anywhere."

Literary life is in full swing online. Discussions and arguments become life-and-death struggles. Literary generals are confirmed and then dethroned.

And still the same incompetence and illiteracy persist.

The same lack of memory.

* * *

It's difficult for a writer to name their books. Some believe that that the title should reflect the essence of the work. Others say that it has to convey the book's mood, its feeling, some motif that the author finds important. In ancient times, Hebrew books got their titles from the first word of their texts.

* * *

"Poetry is the prayer of the soul." This quote from Aleksandr Blok illuminates much: why a poet often approaches unraveling the secrets of the universe, why truly nobody needs "middling" poems.

But don't Blok's words apply to prose and to drama and to criticism too?

* * *

In his article about *Long Conversations* the mathematician and poet Boris Kushner wrote that he read my book while listening to Beethoven's String Quartet No. 15 in A-minor.

I took this as a great compliment. I myself, however, never listen to music while reading. Perhaps in order to submerge myself in the text, I want to hear the music that is always playing in poetry, prose, and drama. That is, of course, if it's true literature. But I do often listen to music while writing. Music allows me to open up my consciousness to the world, to fully sense my own inner freedom... I usually go for Vivaldi, Mozart, Beethoven.

* * *

S. Sh. Compares emigration to death. Not because emigration is difficult and tragic, but because when relocating to a new country you are in process of dying and being reborn as a new person.

"I am so different now..."

She worked at the museum as a tour guide and as a translator back in Lithuania. In Spain, she became a wife and a nanny. Her husband, Joseph-Maria (a painter, 60 years old), became immobile after a car accident. First, he moved about in a wheelchair; now he doesn't move at all.

"...but love conquers all... And I have no regrets. The first year I missed Vilnius terribly. Now it's all so far away from me."

"At first, I felt as if I couldn't get by without my books and things. Now it feels like I don't need any of them at all... even the books. I bought new books, a whole book case-worth."

* * *

I surveyed many people very carefully before coming to the conclusion that as a rule nobody recognizes themselves in the mirror.

In different years I *don't recognize* myself in different ways.

When I was young, I would be startled, not able to comprehend: who's standing in front of me? It seems that my inner field of vision was constructing a different image.

Now, my *non-recognition* is different. Alas, I'm growing disinterested in the man in the mirror.

* * *

By contrast, it's interesting to observe how young people greet you. At times there is a secret craftiness lurking in their eyes. They're thinking about the future—about yours and their own. They seem to know that ahead of you lie illness and death. They, on the other hand... they will be able to trick old age (as a child I was sure that if not I myself, then certainly someone else will soon invent the elixir of life).

Generations make the same mistake over and over again. A few decades fly by in an instant—in the endless bustle of activity. And now it's a new group of *young people* greeting their elders with the same crafty look in their eyes, trying to hide the sympathy, remorse or even light contempt in their gaze.

* * *

I never met her in person. But once I published an essay about E. R.'s sincere, often striking poems. We hadn't communicated for ten years, either on the phone or in letters. Then one day I asked her: "Could I read some new pieces you've written?" E. was silent. I rephrased my question: "Do you still write poetry?" Still silence. Then, she answered—carefully, afraid that I wasn't going to understand her: "I have a different relationship to poetry now. Poems often prophesy unhappiness and always bring sorrow."

In reality, the passing years fell on top of E like mounds of snow. Now she lives in Israel, continuing her yearslong profession of publishing other people's books. "What about your own?" I insist, tactlessly. "Why bother? Everything has already been said in the Holy Books; all of our fates are there already."

She's wrong to assume I wouldn't understand her.

* * *

Happiness is living in harmony with your own soul, which in turn means to fulfil God's plan. Each one of us has been sent to this earth with some mission. But alas we don't often know what it is. Oftentimes by the end of our lives we already know what we're going to die from, but still can't guess why were brought into the world.

* * *

I am impressed by K. N., who has published fifteen books in emigration. He goes to the offices of doctors, lawyers, goes to veteran support groups. And everywhere he begins to read aloud excerpts from his long poems. Does his reading interfere with people working? Of course. But he doesn't leave, even when he's shown the door: "Help me publish my book! Every penny counts..." Oh, if only he had a bit of talent! (1998)

* * *

Here's the same question, rephrased: what is the meaning of human life? Different people will answer this question in their own ways. The most banal answer is to win fame and fortune. That kind of person is destined to lose it all in the end. Even if their dreams come true. I don't need to rehash any of this—I'll merely quote Erich Fromm, whose wise words I often think on: "Humans' main goal in life is to give themselves life. To become what they have the potential to become. The most important fruit to bear is one's own personhood."

* * *

In an interview for the anniversary issue Germany émigré journal *Khreshchatyk* I am asked: "How would describe the position of the Russian language in contemporary literature?" I begin answering with a question of my own: what do you mean by "contemporary literature?" It has been long noted that there are multiple different literatures written in Russian, each with its own parallel life. One of them—the one everyone knows—is represented in the (democratic) journals published in the capitals and is well-appreciated by literary prize committees. Another one bubbles away online. A third—alas, not always noticed by literary criticism—lives in emigration. I'll stop my list there. Because I only want to talk about émigré literature, the eternal Cinderella at someone else's ball. Its Russian is intact, rest assured. Soviet literary scholarship grimly noted that the Russian language in emigration gets frozen over without a "fount of the people's life experience" to draw from. The exception that proved the rule was only made for a few canonical authors that seemed to have taken away some Russian linguistic riches, like a handful of native soil tucked away in the exile's banged up suitcase. But nowadays, you open up the books of Dina Rubina, Grigory Kanovich, Vladimir Porudominsky, Boris Khazanov, Andrey Hazarov, Igor Efimov and are swept away by the sometimes quirky, always vivacious flow of the Russian language.

* * *

Visitors are always keen to ask: how does a writer live in emigration? Do you talk with one another? Nowadays our communications have grown infrequent. Where is the "literary sphere" located now? Where are the traditional centers of the Russian émigré community that had previously been in Paris, Prague, Berlin? They've practically disappeared. In the

US as well. Writers from different countries no longer connected through émigré journals anymore.

As the years pass, I prefer to communicate with my colleagues over the phone. This approach has an undeniable advantage: the voice, much like the soul, doesn't age.

* * *

Many people, writers included, spend a lot of time on social media. Sometimes I think that social media make us go deaf, drowning out the quiet voice of God.

* * *

In May 2018 I saw Havana, Cuba, a city destroyed by communists.

It seemed that many of streets in the center of town were recently destroyed by bombing. Now and again, mournful skeletons appeared out from once beautiful buildings with half-broken walls, windows without glass. It was incredible that there were still people that lived in some of these dead houses. There seemed to be no attempts at repairing them, no scaffolding set up. "Repair or even just a paint job is very expensive," said the tour guide, as if apologizing. But nobody asked her any "provocative" questions. In the bus besides my wife and me sat Cuban émigrés or their descendants. They already knew it all. Thank God that recently they were granted the right to come here from the States — for vacation, but more importantly to see their families.

All the most interested parts of Havana were connected to its damned prerevolutionary past. We spent a long time walking around the old cemetery. It had its own little streets inside. Towering monuments made of granite and marble marked the dates of the areas: 1905, 1934, 1951 etc. In the evening we went to the famous variety show theater "Tropicana" to see a show that had been running continuously since 1939. The communists left it untouched. The singers and dancers were incredible, but their outfits were old and tattered — the government didn't have resources for them.

In the evening there were also no lights in the city. The citizens were saving the electricity. The rain fell hard. Despite the rain, sex workers, mostly old and worn down by their profession, would approach the male tourists. Of course, I remembered the reputation that the resorts and brothels of Havana once had.

Everything passed. When we stepped off our ship, we were considerately warned: "Don't forget to bring toilet paper."

* * *

The role of literature in today's world is small and insignificant. But does that have to upset us? Doubtful. It's a lot worse when literature becomes a "textbook for life." Of course, writers help us understand the world and ourselves, our purpose on this earth. This task, however, is often taken up by philosophy, by psychology, and, most importantly, by religion. Literature, first and foremost, is a magical "glass bead game" played by the few. Let it stay that way.

* * *

Looking in the mirror, I always recognize my eyes.

Gray, with little red veins, their light nearly extinguished. But still *seeking* something.

2018–2020

From the cycle
"The Experience
of Parting"

Passerby

Eighteen years ago, I was shy and unsociable. I had already started dating, but I was never fully vulnerably with any girlfriend, nor even with some of my male friends. However, the third day after I met my future wife, I told her with unqualified certainty: "We live in a fascist country."

I didn't think my words required supporting evidence. Regina didn't ask for any. It was the end of October. Paying no heed to the rain now and then relentlessly flooding the sidewalks, we wandered the streets and swapped our life stories.

Suddenly the rain intensified. I hurried led my companion to the canteen at the riverside train station. I loved coming there because the station reminded me of all the places I would travel to in years to come. We drank our coffees. Besides us, there were two young men sitting at the canteen, arguing about something. One of them, cheerless and stubborn, was attempting to convince his friend:

"You'll see, no one's going to come to my funeral."

Later that evening, listening to the anguished wail of the wind insistently knocking at my window, I wrote this phrase down in my notebook.

* * *

One evening soon after, as we were walking along the riverbank, we encountered an unusual passerby. His long black coat was unbuttoned, his gray hair unfurling in the wind. He approached me and gave me a small hug, politely bowing to

Regina. "This is Pavel Solomonovich," I told her when the passerby was far out of earshot.

Years ago, Vitaly Popov, a feature writer for an Omsk youth magazine, had exclaimed with great enthusiasm: "This is Pavel Solomonovich Dvorkin!" Vitaly wrote skillfully-crafted stories, which, it seemed, subtly but also obviously and much to the displeasure of his editors betrayed the influence of Hemingway. Later, when we met at some dinner, he confessed to me with a shy dreaminess: "If I published a book, I could die happy." Vitaly's book came out during perestroika, but he, alas, had died much earlier. "Pavel Solomonovich," I kept repeating to myself that rainy evening...Vitaly didn't speak of many people with warmth and never spoke of anyone with such reverence.

It turned out Dvorkin had been reading my pieces in the Omsk papers—my essays, theater and film reviews. He made sure that I got his phone number through a mutual acquaintance, generously opening up the doors of his home to me.

* * *

It was a strange home. Due to an architect's error, what should have been a typical one-bedroom apartment had a huge, dark entryway, which the tenants gladly used as a living room. The apartment was clearly meant for young or lonely residents: it didn't have a bedroom. And yet it was inhabited by two old people.

On the wall hung an old photo portrait of Dvorkin himself. His gray eyes gazed ahead without faltering. He wore a military service shirt with two big rhombuses in his buttonholes. Lieutenant general, as we'd say now. Everything became clearer after Dvorkin showed me his memoirs: Years Torn Out of Life.

Perhaps this meeting would be our last. We were half a century apart in age. Yet we irrefutably shared an insatiable interest in Jewishness, Judaism, in our shared roots, which Pavel Solomonovich had lost and I had yet to fully claim.

Like the majority of Soviet Jews from his generation, Dvorkin was a "committed internationalist" (this was a set phrase appearing in obituaries and textbooks). In his youth, he thought a lot about the "reforging" of a person building a new society. But the state's bestial anti-Semitism forced him to think about the fate of the Jewish people and brough him closer to Jewish culture. He knew Yiddish well since he was a child and now had started to learn Hebrew.

...Nevertheless, I want to remember him with a smile. Opening up his newspaper, Pavel Solomonovich often tried to read between the lines, often to comic effect. He scrutinized the lists of candidates for office, the laureates of various prizes and awards — such lists were often published back then. Pencil in hand, he would mark "Jews without a doubt" and "possibly Jews." In his lists, he tried to catch "tendencies." This mental labor was typical for the Jewish intelligentsia during the era of stagnation.

My movement to Jewishness was intuitive. In my family nobody ever reminded me that I was Jewish. My classmates at school would remind me with threats, at times realized without fear of consequences. Later on, I would seek out rare collections of translations from Yiddish and Hebrew in bookstores and reread the novels of Feuchtwanger... Though I could have had an excellent home tutor in Judaism. My dad had studied at a heder, read and wrote in Yiddish freely. He was quiet, modest, and endlessly kind. After lunch, he would go on a neighborhood walk to feed its hungry dogs. However, in this instance, his kindness came through as unexpected harshness. I was silent around him about my desire to discover my Jewish roots. But my father easily recognized the undeniable signs of this desire. And it made him furious. He had told me nothing about the story of his big family, which had for some reason moved from Mogilev to Siberia before the war. Perhaps parts of this story could prove dangerous for his son. "One must be an internationalist!" my father would remind me, at times with care, at other times with menace in his voice. About twenty years later I wrote an essay about the founder of Lithuanian culture Kristijonas Donelaitis. There I formulated a simple truth for myself, which my dad would have, of course, also agreed with: "Different peoples have different roots, but share the same sky."

"Young man," Dvorkin would tell me over the phone, "I have something that might interest you." This was a code we both understood. We met up often, something a few times a week. But I never saw anyone else come to his apartment. During out meetings sometimes Dvorkin's wife Sofia Grigorievna would be a silent presence. She was one of those rare people who are shamed of being part of the intelligentsia, tried to hide it. She had studied at an Institute for Noble Ladies (such institutes, it turns out, continued to exist in many large cities across Russia even after the October Revolution) and knew multiple European language. But after her husband's arrest, she easily put herself in the service of her family, working hard to find ways to support them and raise her two daughters. During the time I would hang out with Dvorkin, Sofia Grigorievna worked as a cashier at the neighboring vegetable market and seemed to be happy with her lot in life.

As a result, Pavel Solomonovich and I would forget that we were trying to learn Hebrew together. More accurately, it became our homework that we would often fail to complete. We spent our time chatting, discussing the news we had heard on the BBC or Voice of America. The news we heard clearly and logically sketched out the system of killing individuality the Soviet Union had created. I labeled this system with a concept I was already familiar with—fascism. Pavel Solomonovich had lived within this System for many long decades. Sometimes I would ask myself: how would he behave if he changed places with his investigator? It was painful to think about this, but I didn't want to idealize my older friend... However, the Stalinist camps were an excellent "reeducation" program. Without any sentimentality, Dvorkin began to recall his youth, given away for the building of the System. My wife's aunt, another "old party member," told many years later, in Israel: "You know, I miss my old party." Dvorkin, on the other hand, recalled only infrequently his service in a squadron dedicated to fighting bandits in the Transbaikal, the intelligence network he created in the Far East, and his work in the organs of the Unified Stated Political Department in different cities across the country. His last place of service was as the head of criminal investigation in Kazakhstan. He was fired from this job in May of 1937, sharply lowered in rank, demoted to working for the people's commissariat of finances. Before finally getting arrested.

He spent seventeen years in prison and exile. In Ukhta and Vorkuta, he worked in the mines, loaded timber, and built the Ukhta-Krutaya highway...After the camps, Pavel Solomonovich returned to his hometown Omsk. Because he was a party member since 1924, he was given a quiet leadership role: the manager of a movie theater. At that time, Dvorkin began writing his memoirs. I was drawn to the author's belief, obvious yet never stated outright, that nothing was the result of individual action. He was not surprised by the phantasmagorical nature of fates and chance meetings. In the camps, he met the former major who had signed the order for his arrest: "I didn't feel any animosity towards him." In interrogation rooms, in camp barracks, in hospital wards, the memoirist recognized the true essence of different people: the "sitting hens" assigned to him; those did not break and those who were driven mad by pangs of conscience; those who didn't hold up under torture and slandered themselves and other... (Dvorkin himself had admitted his "guilt," though the investigator had broken his spine with a glass pitcher).

It was now impossible to publish these memoirs. The thaw had ended. Pavel Solomonovich sent the manuscript to Yevgeny Yevtushenko. The famous poet responded with a warm letter: my wife and I were reading your book all night, passing the pages between one another...

Through the years his gaze remained sharp, and he never lost his ability to "see through" people immediately. Pavel Solomonovich died in the spring of 1974. His family organized a farewell banquet. That's when I remembered what that sullen young man in the train station canteen had said: "You'll see, no one's going to come to my funeral." This room was full. I was sitting at a table with a young man I didn't know. After a shot of vodka, we both started recalling our meetings with the deceased. I had thought Dvorkin lived alone, didn't talk with that many people. My new acquaintance, an engineer at a big factor, immediately destroyed this perception. Pavel Solomonovich had asked him questions all about the life he barely knew anymore. He would arrange their meetings over the phone, strictly demanding him to "stick to the schedule." Dvorkin was an excellent conspirator, the one thing he agreed to take with him from his past life.

Of course, Pavel Solomonovich explained to me the meaning of our mysterious meeting that day on the Irtysh riverbank. After his time in Vorkuta, he was best by horrible bouts of pain, mostly coming at night. For a time, he had worked at a camp hospital and so had a limited knowledge of anesthesia. He even had his own scrip. Pavel Solomonovich walked out onto the street in morning or evening and almost ran under the unyielding wind coming from the river. He was not afraid of the cold and didn't wear gloves even during the bitterest cold. Being quite physically strong (the Vorkuta "miner's conditioning"?), he wasn't afraid of anyone. He told me about this one hooligan he had repelled, much to the young man's shock.

But I never saw Dvorkin again on the Omsk riverbank. Perhaps because, having gotten married soon after, I stopped going there.

Negatives Keep Forever

Back when I lived in Omsk—nearly half a century ago—I published articles with the newspaper Young Siberian. It was only here, in America, where I discovered, to my amazement, that the Young Siberian was no more. I remember all of the paper's staff, their pieces as they appeared on the publication's grayish pages. Among all the young journalists, I most vividly recall the photojournalist Eduard Isakovich Savin, a short, portly, always smiling man. Considerably older than the other staff members, he was nearly always silent—as if he knew something better left unspoken. An immeasurable weariness quietly lived in the depths of his big Jewish eyes. At the same time, he was quick off the mark, frequently making trips all around the entire Omsk Oblast (a region bigger than some European countries). It seemed that every person he encountered on his way deeply interested him.

A paradox: the friends of my youth were often significantly older than me. I easily became friends with Savin. Sometimes he and I would travel to his shoot locations together. We would often end up sitting late into the night in a lonely little apartment—Savin's first marriage had recently fallen apart. While we were drinking tea, he would suddenly, without an obvious logical connection, begin telling me about his travels around the whole wide world.

After I left Omsk to teach at Kemerovo State University, I often visited my hometown—my mom was still living there. And every time I would end up meeting with Savin.

I was always enraptured by his photographs: his camera mysteriously was able to thoughtfully peer into a person's soul. Maybe that's why I was so pleased to receive (in Chicago) his photo album published by the Omsk-based press Rus'.

The album surprised me in many ways. First of all—by some miracle?—it didn't get lost in the mail. Second, it conformed to high Western standards for photography. But more than anything, I was surprised by Savin's fate and work, which had suddenly reemerged before me.

Now (don't be lazy, just Google him) people write of him: "the chronicler of his epoch," "the patriarch of photographs"; his shots are "timeless," "unique black-and-white portraits," depicting "a natural extraordinariness." And yet for many decades Savin worked as a rank-and-file photojournalist for local newspapers in Tyumen, Omsk, the Komi Republic... Unassumingly, without arousing any jealousy, he was the best of all his colleagues—but only that. Thankfully, in the post-Soviet period, cultural historians of the Russian provinces looked back, discovering many talented artists for the first time. Amid what they found were Savin and his poignant works.

His first solo exhibition took place when he was eighty. Soon came his first photo album. His second (the one I received) was titled a little too modestly A Photographer by Calling. However, the title accurately conveyed the essence of his creative life.

The book contains a few collected essays (by Nikolaev, Kem), which allow the reader to look into the artist's laboratory and biography.

Eduard Savin (real surname Merlis) was born in 1925 in Moscow. In 1937, his father was subject to the Stalinist purges. At sixteen, after getting into a fight with his stepfather, he ran away from home, wandering around Central Asia. From there, at seventeen, he volunteered to serve in the army. He wasn't stationed in Tashkent, as the old stories about Soviet Jews go, but rather took part in the crossing of the Dnepr. He fought in the famous "Katyush" regiment and was seriously wounded. Among other awards, he received the Medal "For Courage," a medal those who fought in Tashkent did not receive.

Savin got into photography at the age of eight, in the Moscow Pioneer House. Yes, I now see that he got truly lucky twice. First, he survived the war. Second, his talents were accurately recognized at an early age. This self-awareness, always inherent to talent, prevents a person from walking away from themselves, always loudly reminding them about the most important task in their lives. Here's one example: "One time Savin confessed that nearly every day of the war, he would mentally photograph the burnt villages and heat-lightning from the firing of rocket launchers, the silver ripples of the frigid Oder River, and the unfamiliar gothic style of German cities. And the road where like a steamrolled cat lay the thin pancake of a corpse, a person alive only yesterday, now flattened by heavy vehicles" (Nikolaev).

Savin had taken thousands of photographs. Here are only a few. Siberian landscapes (I still see them in my dreams sometimes); little Polish towns, attracting you with their indistinct mystery; little village boys, unaware of their future; his beloved wife, Tatiana Sergeevna Bibergal (I was the one who introduced the two); famous actors, writers, artists; old men no one knew; lovers who always look like. Not a single staged shot, as researchers would later note.

He remained restless to his very death. At ninety, he continued to Skype me, resolutely oblivious to the time difference between Omsk and Chicago. No, let me try again: he was and remained a relentless seeker of truth, which he entrusted only to his photographs.

Somewhere I read that Eduard Savin donated his entire massive archive to the Museum of Omsk Art. I immediately felt a sense of relief and recalled the words often emblazoned on plaques above prerevolutionary photo studios: "Negatives keep forever."

Yevsey Tseytlin — a writer of prose, a cultural historian, a literary scholar and critic. He is the author of many books published in Russia, America, Lithuania and Germany. These are collections of stories and tales about people of the arts, essays, and monographs. In the last 25 years, nearly all of Yevsey Tseytlin's books have the subtitle *From Diaries of These Years* (*Long Conversations in the Expectation of a Happy Death, From Where to Where* and others). They capture the complex problems of the Jewish consciousness, person and voice on the roads of the Exodus. Tseylin was born in Omsk, Russia, in 1948. He graduated from the department of journalism of the Ural University (1969) and the Higher Literature Courses at the A. M. Gorky Literature Institute (1989). He taught the literary history and culture at higher educational institutions and was the chief editor of the almanac *Jewish Museum* (Vilnius). He got his PhD in philology in 1978 and became an assistant professor in 1980. Beginning in 1968, he was published in many literary and artistic journals and collections. He emigrated twice — to Lithuania and the USA. He has been living in Chicago since 1996 and is the editor of the Chicago monthly *Shalom*.

He was a member of the USSR Writers' Union (1978) and is a member of the Moscow Writers' Union, the Lithuanian Writers' Union, the Russian Writers' Union, and a member of the International Pen Club ("Writers in Exile").

Venya Gushchin is a PhD Candidate at Columbia University, writing a dissertation on the late styles of Russian Modernist poets. He is also a translator, who has worked primarily on Silver Age poetry (Anna Akhmatova, Vladimir Mayakovsky, Aleksandr Blok among others). His translations of Vladimir Mayakovsky have received the Columbia University Slavic Department Pushkin Prize. *Blockade Swallow,* selected poems by Olga Berggolts translated by Gushchin, appeared from Smokestack Books in 2022. His writing has appeared in *Cardinal Points*, *The Birch*, and elsewhere.

Notes

1. The Pamyat Society (National Patriotic Front "Memory") was a Russian neo-Nazi and ultranationalist organization.
2. Armenian pogrom in Baku—ethnic conflict in Baku, capital of Azerbaijan, January 13–20, 1990, accompanied by mass violence towards the local Armenian population: robberies, murders, arson, destruction of property.
3. Rabbi Adin Steinsaltz (1937–2020)—a leading Israeli rabbi, Talmudist, Kabbalist, translator of the Talmud into Modern Hebrew, English, Russian, and Spanish. Founder of the Harry Fischel Institute for Talmudic Research.
4. The pogrom in Kishnev was one of the most well-known pogroms in the Russian Empire. Condoned by the state, it took place on 19–20 April 1903 in Kishnev. 50 people were killed in the pogrom, with 600 wounded and one third of all buildings in the city tarnished.
5. Yuri Vladimirovich Andropov was a Soviet official. General Secretary of the CPSU (head of state) 1982–1984. Head of the KGB 1967–1982.
6. Isaak Emmanuilovich Babel' (1894–1940) was a classic of Soviet literature, famous for his cycles of compact short stories about the Russian Civil War (*Red Cavalry*) and Jewish Odesa (*Odesa Tales*). Repressed by Stalin and executed.
7. Yakov Efimov Elsberg (real surname: Shapirstein; 1901–1976) was a Soviet literary scholar and critic, Ph D. Recipient of the Stalin Prize (1950).
8. The *Kitzur Shulchan Aruch* ("abbreviated Shulchan Aruch" lit. "A little set table") is a collective name for a series of Halakha codices, composed by various authors. The books comprise an abbreviated version of the *Shulchan Aruch*, written by Joseph Karo in the 16th century. This work enumerates influence Halakha injunctions for all aspects of a person's life: prayer, trade, marriage, the rearing of children etc. Jews, wishing to practically follow the injunctions of the Torah, typically follow the *Shulchan Aruch*.

[9] The Blockade of Leningrad was a military blockade of the city of Leningrad (now St. Petersburg) by German, Finish, and Spanish (Blue Division) forces during World War II. It lasted from September 8th, 1941 to January 27th, 1944 — a total of 872 days.

[10] Konstantin Vorob'ev (1919–1975) was a Russian writer, famous for his novella "Here came the giant..." (1971).

[11] *Spring on Zarechnaya Street* (1956, dir. Felix Mironer and Marlen Khutsiev, Odesa Film Studio) was one of the most popular Soviet melodramas.

[12] Founded in the 18th century, the Mariinsky Theater is one of the main musical theaters of Russia and the entire world.

[13] Irena Veisaitė (1928–2020) was a Soviet and Lithuanian literary and theater scholar and critic. Survivor of the Kaunas ghetto. Recepient of a number of Lithuanian and international prizes for her activism.

[14] Writer's Houses (also translated Houses of Creativity) were a network of group vacation homes for writers (i.e. members of the Writer's Union) and their families.

[15] The "enemy of the people" was used in the USSR from 1917 to designated all ideological enemies of the states, i.e., counterrevolutionaries. As General Secretary of Communist Party, Joseph Stalin often noted that in the process of building communism, class struggle was intensifying. This intensification creates a new generation of class enemies, counterrevolutionaries, spies, and saboteurs, all of them deemed to be enemies of the people. In practice, the search for "enemies of the people" always turned into a weeding out of dissent.

[16] Petr Ustinovich Brovka (1905–1980) was a Soviet Belarusian translator, playwright, and public writer.

[17] Vankarem Valer'yanovich Nikiforovich (1934–2011) was a Belarusian, Russian, and American critic and art historian.

[18] Iza (Isaak Davydovich) Kharik (1898–1937) was a Soviet Jewish poet, public writer, and activist, writing mostly in Yiddish.

[19] Lev Platonovich Karsavin (1882–1952) was a Russian religious philosopher, Medievalist historian, poet.

[20] Nikolai Konstantinovich Roerich (1874–1947) was a Russian painter, writer, mystic philosopher, traveler, archeologist, activist, member of the Russian Imperial Academy of Arts (1909).

[21] Mikalojus Konstantinas Čiurlionis (1875–1911) was a composer and artist, an influential part of Lithuanian culture.

[22] Hirsch Osherovich (1908–1994) was a Jewish poet, writing in Yiddish. Faced state repression in the USSR. In 1971, he repatriated to Israel. Recipient of numerous literary prizes.

[23] Osip Emil'evich Mandelstam (1891–1938) was one of the most significant Russian poets of 20th century. A victim of Stalinist repression.

[24] Yuri Nikolaevich (Nasonovich) Tynianov (1894–1943) was one of the leading theorists of Russian Formalism as well as a prose writer, playwright, translator, literary scholar and historian.

[25] Georgy Gurdzhiev (1866–1949) is a Russian philosopher with Greek and Armenian heritage, a mystic, spiritual leader, writer, composer, traveler, and unwilling émigré. His life activities were dedicated to defining a path for a human's self-development, the growth of their consciousness and being in everyday life. His teachings have been retrospectively referred to as the "fourth way."

[26] Dina Il'inichna Rubina (1953 — present) is a Russian-Israeli novelist and short story writer. Her works have been published in the Soviet Union and Russia, translated into numerous languages, and have been made into films. Currently, the Moscow-based publishing house Eksmo is putting out a 24-volume edition of her collected works.

[27] Anatoly Simonovich Liberman (1937 — present) is a Soviet and American linguist, literary scholar, poet, translator, and critic. In 1975, he emigrated to the United States. He currently lives in Minneapolis and works as a professor at the University of Minnesota.

[28] Yuri Karlovich Olesha (1899–1960) was a Soviet Russian novelist, screenwriter, poet, playwright, and journalist. His most famous works include the novel-fairytale *The Three Fat Men* (1924) and the novel *Envy* (1927). In 1930, Olesha composed the play *A List of Assets*, in which the main heroine writes down the good deeds and crimes of the Soviet government in her notebook. Afterwards, Olesha's works were denied publication for many years.

[29] Roman Vershgub (1938–2013) was a doctor and prose writers. Author of *The Living Incomparable* (Chicago, 2017).

[30] Efim Petrovich Chepovitsky (1919–2014) was a Soviet children's author and playwright.

[31] Oleg Anatol'evich Korostelev (1959–2020) was a Russian literary historian, archivist, bibliographer, specializing in Russian émigré circles.

[32] Eduard Bagritsky (1895–1934) was a Russophone Soviet poet, born in Odesa.

[33] Kristijonas Donelaitis (1714–1780) was a Lithuanian poet, Lutheran pastor, and the founder of modern Lithuanian literature. Author of the long poem *Four Seasons*. An 18th century forerunner to the Realist Movement in literature.

[34] Tomas Venclova (1937 — present) is a Lithuanian poet, translator, literary scholar, essayist, dissident, and human rights activist. One of the founders of the Lithuanian Helsinki Group (1976). Emigrated from the Soviet Union in 1976 on invitation by University of California, Berkeley, losing his Soviet citizenship. Professor emeritus of Slavic languages and literatures at Yale University.

[35] Anna Andreevna Akhmatova (born Gorenko) (1889–1966) was Russian Silver Age poet, a translator and literary scholar, one of the most significant figures in the history of 20th century Russian literature. Faced repression from Soviet authorities. Twice nominated for the Nobel Prize in Literature.

[36] Jokabus Josade (1911–1995) was a Lithuanian playwright, prose writer, and critic, the protagonist of Yevsey Tseytlin's *Long Conversations in the Anticipation of a Happy Death*.

[37] Vasily Vasilievich Rozanov (1856–1919) was a Russian religious philosopher, impressionistic writer. The founder of an original literary form.